FOOTBALL
FOOTB...
RIVA...

NEWCASTLE
UNITED
VS
SUNDERLAND

Classic
TYNE &
WEAR
Derby Games

First published in 2012

A catalogue record for this book is available from the British Library

ISBN: 978-0-857331-78-6

Published by Haynes Publishing, Sparkford, Yeovil,
Somerset BA22 7JJ, UK
Tel: 01963 442030 Fax: 01963 440001
Int. tel: +44 1963 442030 Int. fax: +44 1963 440001
E-mail: sales@haynes.co.uk
Website: www.haynes.co.uk

Haynes North America Inc., 861 Lawrence Drive, Newbury Park, California 91320, USA

Images © Mirrorpix

Creative Director: Kevin Gardner
Designed for Haynes by BrainWave

Printed and bound in the US

NEWCASTLE
UNITED
VS
SUNDERLAND

Classic
TYNE &
WEAR
Derby Games

Paul Days

This book is dedicated to the memory of

George Summerside
30th August 1958 – 8th January 2012

"Life is God's novel. Let him write it."
Isaac Bashevis Singer

CONTENTS

INTRODUCTION

It's the game that everyone wants to see and it excites the football fan from the moment the fixture list comes out. It's the one most likely to cause civil disorder and to have its roots in some facet of a country's, city's or region's society and history. It is, of course, the football "derby" game.

From Argentina to Zambia, each country affiliated to FIFA – football's governing body – will have a fixture or fixtures that provoke the reasonable and the unreasonable citizen into a feeling of mutual loathing for the opposition supporter, who may be known or unknown to them, for the duration of the match or perhaps permanently. At times it defies belief and all rational norms.

Argentina has the famous Boca Juniors versus River Plate fixture, a game rooted in the poor–rich divide in Buenos Aires. In Glasgow, Scotland, there is the Rangers and Celtic match that has its roots in religious conflict.

But in the northeast of England there is a football rivalry as intense as anywhere in the world, a rivalry that goes back as far as the English Civil War, nearly 400 years ago. It doesn't just have a sporting background: it has an industrial and political one. Two communities collide. Society may have changed and the method of sorting out disputes and enmity may have altered, but, in its essence, this football rivalry is a continuation of a battle that commenced in the 17th century with Oliver Cromwell and King Charles I.

Needless to say, that rivalry is between Newcastle United FC and Sunderland AFC – the Tyne–Wear derby game.

In the writing of this tale the matches themselves don't do the story justice. Inevitably there are unpalatable events to be related that provide a context to the nature of the rivalry. We have done our best in this book to approach such matters sensitively and factually.

Facts, however, when it comes to the Geordies (Newcastle United) and the Mackems (Sunderland), are always arguable – a contradiction that cannot be explained. Even monumental defeats for one side or the other can easily be justified, to ensure that neither club is seen as weak in the face of the "enemy". Neither team ever beats the other; it merely gains an upper hand that will be rectified the next time they meet.

For people who do not like football, or even for those who do, some of the events that surround this fixture provoke widespread disapproval. They have potentially far-reaching consequences for the local communities and individuals, making it imperative that authorities such as the police regard the games with heightened importance.

When the games are over, the games aren't over – another contradiction. Go to towns such as Chester-le-Street in County Durham, South Shields, the City of Durham, for example, mainly near the border of Tyne and Wear and County Durham, and you will find social disorder in the aftermath of the game is common and often expected, and the sound of police sirens can fill the air. Communities split 50/50; and when you add alcohol and throw in testosterone, you get an inevitable cocktail of violence.

What sets the Newcastle v Sunderland rivalry apart from other football derby games is that the two teams don't even come from the same city. They are situated 12 miles apart. It might as well be a million miles, such are the differences in attitude between the two sets of fans.

Those that live within the Sunderland city boundaries have had their enmity towards Newcastle stoked by such events as the transfer of the seaside city into the newly created Tyne and Wear county in 1974, following the 1972 Local Government Act. This unpopular move saw Sunderland leave County Durham. Annoyance even extended to the building of the Tyne & Wear Metro public transport system in 1980, which initially served Tyneside but not Wearside – rightly or wrongly the people of Sunderland considered that they had contributed to it for 22 years through local taxes and received nothing in return. The facility was extended east towards the North Sea in 2002.

The rivalry extends to absurdity, with some fans of Newcastle United reportedly refusing to eat bacon, due to its red-and-white colouring, whilst the popular breakfast cereal Sugar Puffs is still boycotted by many Sunderland fans due to the fact that the former Newcastle United manager Kevin Keegan was used in one of Kellogg's more famous commercials 20 years ago. Don't tell them about the honey, mummy, in Sunderland.

However, let's not concentrate wholly on the social aspects of the fixture, critical though they are to understanding its place in northeast life and football folklore. The story of the Tyne–Wear derby also tells of marvellous football matches, sublime footballers, electric atmospheres that can only be cut with a very sharp knife and eras long forgotten. The fixture started in Victorian times and is still going strong in the 21st century.

It's black and white (Newcastle United) versus red and white (Sunderland).

Sunderland AFC (SAFC) is the senior club, Newcastle United (NUFC) the junior but, as with a lot of tales in life, sometimes the pupil becomes the master, albeit temporarily. Remember, no one ever truly wins this fixture. What we have here is one big football match that has lasted, so far, for 130 years.

The story, however, starts in 1639.

THE BATTLE OF BOLDON HILL

The Bishops' Wars, which took place in 1639 and 1640, were precursors of the English Civil wars, of which there were three. At the heart of the Bishops' Wars was the intention of the then king, Charles I, to impose Anglican reforms on the Scottish Church, something that was rejected out of hand by the Scots. Angered by this, the king sent an expeditionary force northwards to bring the Scots to heel, but due to financial constraints and a lack of faith in his rabble army they returned to England without a shot being fired.

Despite being chastened by this, Charles I turned to parliament for support; however, the simmering rivalry between the monarchy and parliament was such that the latter rejected the king's pleas for funds to build an army capable of mounting a proper challenge to the Scots. As a result Charles dismissed parliament and marched on Scotland – only to find, much to his surprise, that the English forces were routed by the Scots.

Although Charles I attempted to make peace with parliament, any trust between the parties evaporated on 4th January 1642 when the king's men attempted to arrest five members of parliament. However, they were spirited away prior to the troop's arrival. Charles then left London and raised the Royal Standard in Nottingham in August 1642, placing his troops under the command of the 3rd Earl of Essex. The scene was set for a civil war: Royalists v Parliamentarians.

Most of the country was neutral at the start of the conflict and, indeed, fighting men on each side amounted to only about 13,000.

1

The Royalist support was centred around the north and west of England, and Wales. The Parliamentarians held the more affluent areas of the south and, critically, many of the ports.

The initial battles in the first English Civil War were fought in and around London, specifically Edgehill and Turnham Green. From there, conflict spread to engulf many other parts of the country.

In the northeast of England there was a growing animosity between the peoples of Sunderland and Newcastle. In order to keep the support of the richer Newcastle, Charles had consistently awarded the east of England coal trade rights to the merchants of that city. This effectively impoverished the people in Sunderland, who, as a result, sided with the Parliamentarians (also known as the Roundheads). Something had to give.

In 1643 the Parliamentarians enlisted the help of Scottish soldiers, known as Covenanters, in exchange for the Scots' right to religious freedom, and an agreement called the Solemn League and Covenant was drawn up between the two parties. As a result, on 19th January 1644, the Army of the Covenant crossed the River Tweed and entered England under the command of the Earl of Leven. They headed south towards the Royalist stronghold of Newcastle, intent on taking it for parliament.

However, on 2nd February 1644, the Marquis of Newcastle, William Cavendish, beat them to it, and entered the city from the south with his army from Yorkshire, just hours before the arrival of the Covenanters. One day later the Earl of Leven's request for the surrender of Newcastle was rejected, and a subsequent skirmish took place, with the Scottish forces capturing the outskirts of the city. On 6th February Scottish artillery landed in Blyth port but took two days to reach Newcastle, and on 8th February further skirmishes took place in and around Gateshead.

The Earl of Leven then took stock of the situation and bypassed Newcastle, crossing the Tyne at Ovingham, Bywell and Eltringham, and marching his troops towards the Parliamentary sympathetic town of Sunderland, where he could rest and plan tactics. The Covenanters were welcomed with open arms. On hearing this the Marquis of Newcastle (who died in 1676 and was subsequently buried at Westminster Abbey) left the city undefended and, together with his Royalist army, headed towards Sunderland, intent on routing the Covenanters.

At Penshaw Hill, south of Sunderland, the two armies were set to meet; however, the weather intervened, so Leven returned to Sunderland and the Marquis moved on to another Royalist stronghold – Durham.

In subsequent days the Scots took both South Shields and Chester-le-Street; the latter was a strategically important place from which a march to York, a bastion of monarchist support and the hub of the Marquis' communication with the king, could commence.

Inevitably, a northeast conflict between the Royalist and Parliamentary forces would take place and, on 25th March 1644, the Battle of Boldon Hill was fought. Boldon Hill, for those who don't know the northeast, lies between Newcastle and Sunderland, but nearer to the latter.

Although popular myth has it that the Newcastle forces were routed this wasn't quite the case as the Scots were driven back to the safety of Sunderland by 4,000 of the Marquis' troops and 3,300 Royalist cavalry under the command of Sir Charles Lucas (ironically the Marquis was widely regarded as the finest horseman in Europe at that time). However, the Marquis had a simple choice, continue the defence of Newcastle and lay siege to Sunderland or open up a second front by putting his efforts into securing York, a strategically more important location and one which some of the Covenanters were now marching towards. He chose York, situated in the county where most of his forces were from. However, the Covenanters subsequently took nearby Selby just days after Boldon

Hill, before the Marquis could get there, and once he arrived in York, outnumbered and without support, an endgame was already being played.

By fleeing towards York the Marquis left the City of Newcastle open to conquest and thus the Parliamentarians came out of Sunderland and gained a significant victory. The battles of Stamford Bridge and then Marston Moor took place later that year, near York, which resulted in the Marquis of Newcastle humiliatingly fleeing abroad. He travelled to Hamburg, Amsterdam, Rotterdam, Paris and then on to Antwerp, where, due to his past friendship with people in the city, including the family of the Flemish baroque artist Anthony van Dyck, he settled for a while. The Royalists thus ceased to be a fighting force in the northeast of England. In this way, not only had Sunderland assisted the Parliamentarians in capturing Newcastle, it had also contributed, albeit unwittingly, to the desertion of the Marquis.

In recognition of its loyal service to parliament Oliver Cromwell, himself an MP, transferred many of the coal licences from Newcastle to Sunderland. However, the tale does not end there.

In 1660 what was known as the Restoration took place, effectively reviving the monarchy under King Charles II (and also allowing the Marquis of Newcastle to return to England). Many of the coal licences were given back to Newcastle. What made matters worse for Sunderland was that a local coal cartel, known as the Vend, emerged, and ensured that London received its supply from Newcastle.

Yet in 1814 the vend was fatally underminded by the arrival of Arthur Mowbray. His attempts to modernize the local Vane-Tempest collieries inspired the expansion of the northeast railway network to Sunderland, with a subsequent boom in trade that led, amongst other things, to Sunderland being recognized as the biggest shipbuilding town in the world. Mowbray is acknowledged to this day with a green belt known as Mowbray Park, which is situated near Sunderland city centre.

For those who do not know the northeast of England perhaps an explanation is necessary. The region was exceptionally industrialized and, historically, has at its heart coal mining and shipbuilding. Both the River Tyne (Newcastle) and the River Wear (Sunderland) became crucial to the economic well-being of the region. It's doubtful that any family whose roots belong in the northeast, does not have a member who at some point was either a coal miner for the National Coal Board (NCB) or a shipbuilder for firms such as Austin & Pickersgill (Wearside) or Swan Hunter (Tyneside).

Before we move on it is worth mentioning what appears to be a reported factual inaccuracy in the historical dispute between the two communities. It is often cited that they opposed each other during the Jacobite Rebellion of 1745, which led eventually to the Battle of Culloden. The confusion appears to have arisen due to the belief that the then Duke of Newcastle sided with the monarchy and the then Earl of Sunderland sided with the Stuarts (as represented by the person of Bonnie Prince Charlie). However, the Earl of Sunderland (a subsidiary title of the Duke of Marlborough) was not from Sunderland but from Wiltshire. Furthermore, there is no evidence to suggest that he ever supported the Jacobite cause.

Notwithstanding the confusion over the Jacobite Rebellion, as it stood Sunderland had fought two conflicts against Newcastle, one political and one industrial, and had eventually gained the upper hand in both. However, as we shall see in this enduring battle between the two cities (Sunderland became a city in 1992) victory remains temporary, and in any case Newcastle is widely – albeit arguably – now regarded as the region's capital, so perhaps the latter has had the last laugh after all.

By the time Sunderland AFC was formed, the shipbuilding town that gave birth to it was booming. The formation of Newcastle United would come later and would partially owe its existence to cricket!

A third conflict between the two cities was about to begin and would be played out on a football field rather than a battlefield.

As we know, it still takes place today.

CLUB FORMATIONS

The story chronologically starts with the formation of Sunderland AFC, originally said to be in 1879, but now increasingly believed to be 1880. The sport of cricket pre-dates football in the town by decades, with the local club playing its first recorded game in 1808. Sunderland rugby club was formed in 1873.

It was James Allan, originally from Ayrshire, who founded the Sunderland and District Teachers Association – which became Sunderland AFC – in October 1879, supposedly at the British Day School in Norfolk Street, Sunderland (where the Norfolk Hotel now stands) in the Sunniside area of the city. A teacher since April 1879 at the local Hendon Board School, Allan was the second assistant master. Disappointed at the lack of a round ball game, the legend is that he returned from his summer holiday in his native Scotland with a football, which pupils and masters subsequently kicked around in the schoolyard.

However, a look at the Hendon Board School logbook makes no mention of the founding in October 1879. There were more important matters to record, such as the fact that a circus was in town and many boys were late for school as a result, and that George Burns, a youngster in Sunderland, was to be admitted free of charge until his father found work.

The first we know of the Teachers is an announcement in the local paper which reads:

Saturday October 16 1880, a new club has been formed at Sunderland under the name of Sunderland Teachers Association Football Club.

This club formed by Teachers is not confined to this profession. The Blue House Field at Hendon has been secured. The colours chosen are Navy Blue and it has been decided to join the Northumberland and Durham Association. The team will play in the Challenge Cup competition. Elected Secretary is Mr W Elliott, 4 Rutland Terrace, Sunderland.

In short, if the round ball game did arrive in Sunderland in 1879 it was not acknowledged for 12 months. In an evidence-based world we arrive at the conclusion that Sunderland AFC, as it became, was born in October 1880.

Meanwhile, 12 miles away, the formation of Newcastle United would take a different route from that of Sunderland AFC, and be linked to cricket.

The cricket side of the equation was Stanley Cricket Club; to avoid confusion it is worth pointing out that this was not Stanley in County Durham. The Stanley in question was the cricket club that played on vacant land near Stanley Street in South Byker, a suburb of Newcastle. Following an AGM on 15th November 1881 it was decided to form a sister football club, which played its first football match on 26th November 1881, a 5-0 defeat of Elswick Leather Works 2nd XI. In his book *United: The First 100 Years* the Newcastle United historian Paul Joannou confirms that due to confusion with two other local clubs, Stanley Nops and Stanley Albion, both County Durham teams, Stanley football club changed their name to Newcastle East End in October 1882.

The football side of the Newcastle United equation was made up of two halves. First of all we have Rosewood, who later joined forces with East End, and, secondly, West End FC, who would become Newcastle West End.

West End originally played on a cricket field not far from Town Moor, but in May 1886 they took over the lease at a ground named St James' Park, formerly the pitch of Newcastle Rangers, from the town's freemen.

As in Sunderland, where the senior club battled for supremacy with Sunderland Albion, formed by a disaffected James Allan, a battle for supremacy between the two Newcastle clubs commenced. Competition was heightened by East End's decision to become a limited company in 1890. Whilst West End followed suit, results by 1892 were poor and the club was on the verge of extinction. A deal was therefore struck with East End to lease the St James' Park ground, and West End ceased operation as a football club in May 1892.

East End, however, still had problems to overcome, amongst them, rather remarkably given the Newcastle United supporters' reputation for passion and loyal support – fan apathy. With disappointing crowds, and in an effort to attract more support, radical changes were implemented. One of these was to change the club's name, and with several suggestions noted the club's committee went with Newcastle United. The East End name was changed by legal title on 9th December 1892.

Newcastle United and Sunderland AFC, names that would become synonymous with Association Football, were in business as the sporting institutions we now know.

THE RIVALRY TAKES SHAPE

1879/80 to 1889/90

Since Sunderland AFC was probably formed in 1880 rather than 1879, as we have seen, it is highly unlikely that the game originally accredited as being Sunderland's first, against Ovingham in 1879, took place. No date, result, team line-ups or scorers have ever been recorded.

Assuming this was the case it didn't take long for the Wearsiders to play their first game after their formation when they entertained Ferryhill on 13th November 1880, losing 0-1. A victory over Ovingham followed before the then Blues (Sunderland played in an all blue strip originally, in due deference to their then home, the Blue House Field in Hendon, a working-class area of the town) competed in the Northumberland and Durham Cup, defeating Burnopfield at Rowlands Gill in a second-round replay, following a 2-2 draw at Hendon. This led to a semi-final encounter with Tyneside's Newcastle Rangers at St James' Park in December 1881. The hosts thrashed Sunderland 5-0 – despite the Wearside line-up including the likes of club founder James Allan – in a game that saw the Wearside team play at Newcastle United's present home before the Magpies did.

A return friendly with the Rangers, again at St James' Park, in December 1881, saw the Geordies once more triumph, this time by a much closer margin, 1-0, with the game finishing in semi-darkness. The lack of illumination would presumably have caused a problem for both teams as the Rangers also played in a dark blue strip.

It would be fair, as we shall see, to conclude that in those days the divide between Tyneside and Wearside was as intense as it is nowadays; however, this did not stop players from either side of the 12-mile divide playing for Wearside and Tyneside clubs, with the Sunderland founder James Allan being a case in point. He played for Sunderland, Durham County, Northumberland County and also Rangers. He was an interesting character.

Born in Ayrshire in 1858, Allan attended Glasgow University before coming down to Sunderland to take up a teaching position at Hendon Board School. Here he was the second assistant master, having been appointed in April 1879 at a salary of £60, rising later to £90.

As the founder of Sunderland AFC James Allan was a complex and often unpopular character, but he was successful in his teaching career – so much so that on leaving Hendon Board School he moved on to teaching at Thomas Street School until becoming the headmaster of Hylton Road School, where he stayed until his death in 1911.

He took an active part in football all his life, holding the position of treasurer at the time he left Sunderland AFC, and then, of course, leading the breakaway group that formed Sunderland Albion in 1888, a move that almost saw the death of Sunderland AFC. He was also at one point the chairman of the Wearside League.

He was always a very fit man and attempted to cycle from Sunderland to Glasgow to witness the 5th April 1890 Scotland v England encounter at Hampden Park. He was thwarted when his bike gave up on him at Edinburgh!

As a player he was notionally an outside-left and was a prolific goalscorer. To prove this he holds Sunderland's individual goal-scoring record of 12 in one match, against Castletown in 1884. To counter this he was very often accused of dishing out "rough play" on the opposition in a needless, underhand way. He could also be a selfish ball player, which could leave his team-mates exasperated. Due to his slight physique he was often referred to as "The Boneless Wonder".

However, his footballing exploits were enough for him to be recognized by the Rangers club, who recruited Allan to play for them against the then mighty Queens Park from Glasgow in the 1882/83 season. Although the Rangers team lost, James Allan *"raised cheer after cheer by his determined play, dribbling nearly the whole length of the field time after time"*.

In the 1884/85 season Allan was accused of bribing one of the Birtley backs, Watson, to the tune of £2 to *"play a dummy game"*. Incensed, Allan threatened legal action, in his usual straight-to-the-point, go-for-the-jugular, manner. No further action was taken by Birtley.

Although Allan played in many friendly and Durham Challenge Cup games for Sunderland, his record shows that he featured in just three competitive fixtures for the club, all FA Cup ties, including the club's very first professional match, which was the Redcar Cup tie in November 1884.

James Allan died on 18th October 1911 at his home, 37 Elmwood Street, Sunderland. The death certificate gave his occupation on the date of death as a schoolmaster. His passing was registered in the Sunderland West sub-district by his son, W Allan, on the day he died, with the cause of death given by James Chalmers MD as apoplexy. This is a general medical term given to someone who passes away very quickly from, for example, a sudden heart attack; therefore we know that the Sunderland club founder did not suffer in his passing.

Allan was just 53 years of age.

The rivalry with Newcastle, rather than merely with Tyneside teams in general, commenced on 3rd November 1883 when Sunderland travelled to Byker to play Newcastle East End. It was Sunderland's first victory over a Tyneside team and the 3-0 win by what was effectively a reserve side, set the tone for a number of Wearside triumphs over their Tyneside rivals. This hardly reflected badly on the Newcastle teams as Sunderland were obviously the stronger side in the early years.

In 1882 Newcastle's civic administrators founded a Temperance Festival on the local Town Moor in conjunction with Race Week. The event was a showcase for all that was good in Newcastle and was generally law-abiding (in sharp contrast to the London equivalent), drawing crowds in excess of 200,000 people. Multiple events were on show, including cricket matches, military shows and brass bands as well as games of football. Bizarrely for the northeast such a gathering was characterized by a lack of drunkenness!

It didn't take long for Sunderland to be invited to the Temperance Festival and the first of such encounters took place on 25th June 1884 where, in a game of two 30-minute periods, the visitors once more triumphed over an East End side, this time 3-1.

It was 17 months before Sunderland ventured over to Newcastle again but when they did, in November 1885, they once more triumphed 1-0, this time at Byker. East End had been severely weakened even before the match kicked off when top players Muir, White and Blackett had been called up by Northumberland, who had a match on the same day. Sunderland, however, were also handicapped through the absence of both Allan and McDonald. It was generally agreed by the watching press that East End's Cook had played well.

By now Sunderland were playing in red-and-white halved shirts, in advance of the move to the famous stripes, taking the field in their new kit in December 1884 when they defeated Castle Eden 8-1.

To date it was the East End club that had struck up a rivalry with Sunderland, however, West End played their first match against their Wearside adversaries in February 1886 when they visited Abbs Field (Sunderland had now left the Blue House Field). The hosts won

1-0 with a 60th-minute goal from Erskine following a lovely left-wing cross. The Tyneside team were hardly disgraced when you consider that Sunderland were undefeated in their 12 games against English opposition that season in Fulwell (a district of Sunderland).

One of the hardest fought and most exciting games of Sunderland's season took place the following week at Abbs Field when East End were unlucky not to win, having led through a Muir goal until a late Allan equalizer just three minutes from time. In a game refereed by Sunderland AFC's Reverend Hindle, the match reports told of the first signs of hostility in Tyne–Wear encounters as many of the 1,500 crowd had given the Newcastle players a particularly rough ride while the home team sought an equalizer. Furthermore, in what would become a common theme in early games between sides from Newcastle and Sunderland, *"the unselfish passing and sharpness of East End more than made up for their lack of muscle compared to the home side"*. Sunderland invariably had the larger of the two teams in the 19th and early 20th century, whilst Newcastle relied more on trickery, on this occasion from Scott.

On the subject of trickery it's worth noting that in the 1800s the teams lined up in a very attacking formation. There was no 4-4-2 or 4-3-3, but 1-2-7 and 2-2-6 were popular.

West End played Sunderland no fewer than five times in 1886. The biggest of the encounters, by far, was the first competitive game between a team from Tyneside and Wearside, namely the 30th October 1886 English (FA) Cup tie played at Newcastle Road, Sunderland's new home following their move from Fulwell. It was a titanic struggle, settled 2-1 in Sunderland's favour after extra-time. The crowd, a very large (for the day) 3,500, was treated to an exceptional game of football. In fact the crowd was so big that it caught the administrators off guard and many supporters missed the kick-off.

West End were without Taylor, owing to a family bereavement, and having won the toss the visitors defended the Newcastle Road End. It didn't take long for Sunderland to fall behind when Kirtley, in the home goal, was beaten all ends up after 10 minutes by a lovely Campbell header. However, the lead didn't last long as Lord lofted the ball over Oldham in the visiting goal to equalize *"amidst tremendous cheering"* from the home crowd.

In a keenly contested second half neither side could press home their advantage, and although the home side had the better of the closing stages the game ended 1-1. By now darkness was falling and, as there were no floodlights, the West End players were incensed when the referee, Mr Reed from Cleveland, insisted that as this was an English Cup tie extra-time of two 15-minute periods would be played. In the second period of extra-time Sunderland thought that they had scored a second goal, but owing to the bad light the referee couldn't be sure that the ball had crossed the line – and much to Sunderland's chagrin he ruled out their claim for a goal. However, a sickening twist for the visitors arrived in the 115th minute when Lord scored a second goal, driving the ball home when Duns failed to clear.

West End protested that if Sunderland had not scheduled the game on 30th October – the last possible date on which matches on that round of the English Cup could be played – then a replay would have been possible. However, in what was perhaps the first example of gamesmanship in the Tyne–Wear rivalry, Sunderland knew that the West End team had the more cosmopolitan makeup, having recruited players from outside the Newcastle vicinity, and had wanted to give themselves the best possible chance of winning. In essence the Wearsiders weren't keen on playing West End on their own patch and considered the Tynesiders to have the better team.

Nevertheless, much to Sunderland's dismay West End's complaints were upheld and a replay took place at St James' Park on 13th November. However, this was not before Sunderland lodged a protest at the state of the ground, the complaint being that *"the crossbar of the bottom goal is on a lower level than the centre of the field, also the ground slopes into one corner"*. As most grounds at that time were like this, the appeal was dismissed. Sunderland's fear of West End was well founded as they were taken out of the running for the cup 0-1 when Angus scored after 75 minutes. The visiting cause wasn't helped when Dowk Oliver had to leave the field midway through the second half with a broken collarbone, leaving Sunderland to finish the match with 10 men. As Dowk was notionally a defender it's highly likely that the Sunderland defence, given the tactics of the day, would have been reduced to just one man as the rest of the team screamed forward.

As a postscript to this match West End were courteous enough to agree to and play a benefit game for Oliver at Newcastle Road on 27th November 1886. In those days there was no sickness benefit and Dowk had been relying on family and friends to keep his loved ones warm and fed during his time convalescing.

This was not the first benefit game (now known as a testimonial) for a Sunderland player. That distinction belonged to the 2nd April 1885 match for their fullback Watson, who had been signed from Birtley against an Army XI in Dumfries, Scotland.

A drawn friendly at Newcastle Road against East End one week after the Oliver benefit game was the last of the rivalry for 10 months, until 8th October 1887 and a game at St James' Park against West End that Sunderland won 3-2. However, the talking point wasn't a fine game of football but the poor crowd behaviour, described in the press as follows:

The meeting attracted a great deal of interest and had the day been fine instead of a wretchedly wet and miserable one no doubt the attendance would have been huge. As it was close on 5,000 people assembled including a great many from Sunderland. The crowd was very noisy but one cannot help remarking that supporters would do well to remember that a football match is a game and not a war in which it is necessary to urge men to do each other bodily harm.

This is what a large section of the crowd were doing whilst their language was occasionally disgusting in the extreme. Those mainly responsible were mere lads and something will have to be done to check their behaviour. Few men of sense would be inclined to take their wives, sisters or sweethearts to one of these football matches on account of this vile language emanating from all sides of the ground. The lowest depths were reached at this game and as there is a law against the use of blasphemous and obscene language the West End committee should resist such disgraceful behaviour.

A few extra police and a severe warning as to the intentions of those in authority would have a good effect.

Following on from the extreme partisanship previously shown by the Sunderland supporters towards their Tyneside guests it was evident that a great rivalry was taking shape, and that supporter bad behaviour was simmering.

It was safe to say that the 5th November 1887 English Cup tie between Sunderland and West End at Newcastle Road attracted huge interest. The sight which greeted the visitors when they arrived was long remembered, with the temporary stands erected by the Sunderland committee crowded with a seething black mass of people. Every vantage point was occupied with spectators; they were even on top of the new press box, and neither threats from committee men nor the police could budge them.

Sunderland won the game 3-1 but there was general astonishment at the size of the crowd, which was estimated at 8,000; easily the highest gate ever recorded for a match between Sunderland and either East End or West End at that point in time. This was Sunderland's ninth consecutive victory, and with Blackburn

Rovers up next it was evident that Sunderland were on their way to becoming a footballing powerhouse.

This encounter saw Sunderland play in red-and-white stripes, just a few weeks after showing their new colours off for the first time to the Wearside public in the 24th September 1887 encounter with Darlington St Augustine's.

There were eight more matches between Sunderland and Newcastle sides during the decade, which were evenly split between East End and West End. Two characteristics emerged from the encounters, which were: Sunderland victories (in five of the games) and two attendances above 10,000, both on Wearside at Newcastle Road.

At Newcastle Road in February 1888 West End recorded a rare win for Newcastle, defeating Sunderland 3-2 with an own goal from the home goalkeeper, Kirtley, setting the visitors on their way back from a 0-2 deficit. The proceeds from the 5,000 crowd were to be given to the Monkwearmouth and Southwick Dispensary, the first, but certainly not the last, charity football match that sides from the two cities would play against each other.

Two months later the two sides met again, this time at St James' Park. As was the annual custom, the winners of the Challenge Cups of Northumberland and Durham met to determine the champions of the north. The game was played alternately in Northumberland and Durham, and this year it was the turn of the Northumberland Cup winners to host the event. While the latter had never registered a victory over their sister county, the previous year Shankhouse (a mining village in Northumberland) had forced a draw with Sunderland. The weather was excellent and a crowd of 6,000 people assembled, producing a tidy sum for the local football association.

Sunderland were not at full strength but nevertheless fielded a good side with the aid of a few reserves, all of whom had figured in the 1st XI at some stage of the season. West End raised eyebrows when they drafted in Hunter and Grant as guests, as neither had played any part in winning the Northumberland trophy. Accounts differ as to where the left-back hailed from, with both Renton and Grantham being quoted in this connection. He had only arrived that morning and was named as J S Haig on the bills (team sheet) but it was generally accepted that his name was Hunter, although one rumour went as far as to name him as Forbes, then an international player.

Drafting in guest players made no difference on the day as Sunderland ran out winners 2-0, with first-half goals from Stewart and Gloag, although it was generally recognized that a string of good saves by Kirtley, the away side's custodian, also contributed to the win.

By now teams from England and Scotland were regularly playing each other but the fixtures were locally arranged and haphazard.

On 20th July 1885, the FA announced that it was *"in the interests of Association Football, to legalise the employment of professional football players, but only under certain restrictions"*. Clubs were allowed to pay players provided that they had either been born or had lived for two years within a six-mile radius of the ground.

This effectively changed the ball game entirely as the decision to legitimately pay players resulted in an increased wage bill. The call for more organized and lucrative football grew louder.

It was in March 1888 that the idea of a regular fixture list was mooted by William McGregor, then a committee member at Aston Villa. The idea was developed further, and after meetings at Anderson's Hotel in London's Fleet Street on 23rd March 1888 and at the Royal Hotel, Manchester, on 17th April 1888, the basis of a league competition was agreed. Invitations to membership of a Football League were sent to 12 clubs, six from Lancashire (Accrington, Blackburn Rovers, Bolton Wanderers, Burnley, Everton and Preston North End) and six from the Midlands (Aston Villa, Derby County, Notts County, Stoke, West Bromwich Albion and Wolverhampton Wanderers).

William McGregor was elected president, Harry Lockett of Stoke was appointed secretary and Major William Sudell of Preston North End was the first treasurer. The annual subscription for each member club was set at two guineas (£2 10s).

Although clubs from Newcastle and Sunderland were not represented initially they would be in time, becoming high-profile, well-supported and successful members. However, what the formation of the Football League did do was to spawn a series of regional leagues, such as the Northern League in the northeast, within which both East End and West End were early successful participants.

Other than cricket, where an intermittent and unreliable County Championship had existed since 1826, the Football League was a first for world sport, certainly for football, and was a format that would be repeated the world over in the years to come.

The November 1888 encounter between Sunderland and East End on Wearside produced little of note in a surprisingly sporting encounter that the home side won, progressing through to the fourth round of the English Cup.

At Chillingham Road one month later East End held Sunderland to a 1-1 draw, although the game was restricted to 30 minutes each way as the away team's train had been unduly delayed and arrived late at Newcastle Central station. Consequently, it was 20 minutes after the advertised start time that the red and whites made it to the Heaton-based ground. As there were no floodlights and it was wintertime the night had closed in quickly, and 45 minutes each way was out of the question.

A significant moment in the history of Tyneside and Wearside football took place in May 1889 when Tom Watson, then secretary (manager) of the East End club, moved to Sunderland AFC, following the assertion by club president Robert Thompson that the latter needed a full-time secretary. The move for Watson was prompted by an application and subsequent rejection for a place in the Football League during the 1888/89 close season.

John Grayston, a founder member of the Sunderland club and also a committee member, knew just the man: Tom Watson. Given £10 and told to bring him back to Ellerslie Terrace (the SAFC HQ), Grayston went to Newcastle and found Tom in a public house. Given the opportunity of assisting Sunderland AFC he jumped at the chance (remember that at that time the Wearsiders were by far the bigger of the northeast clubs), and that evening, resplendent in a new suit, money in his pocket and cleaned up he was presented to the Sunderland committee. He was given a house and a salary of 35 shillings per week.

Watson was a superb man manager and tactician who had begun his administrative career with Newcastle West End, before moving across the city to Chillingham Road in 1888. One of Watson's main strengths lay in the fact that he believed in "Scotch" (Scottish) footballers, who at that time were perhaps the finest on the planet, and, along with committee men from the Newcastle and Sunderland clubs he served, made many trips to Scotland in search of burgeoning young talent, usually top-class internationals. Indeed, one of Watson's first tasks at Sunderland was to recruit Scotsmen such as Johnny Campbell (Renton) and Johnny Auld (Third Lanark); players who would become Wearside football legends.

The last season of the decade, 1889/90, witnessed four encounters between Sunderland and their Newcastle rivals (Sunderland played East and West End twice each). The Tyneside players could manage just two goals between them in those four matches.

By now, though both East End and West End were playing in the inaugural Northern League, Sunderland had bigger fish to fry and was knocking on the door of the Football League.

In the first meeting of the sides in two seasons – against West End in September of 1889 – the Newcastle Road crowd eagerly awaited a look at the Tyneside team's Bob Kelso, the Scottish international signed from Renton, who had won two Scottish Cup medals. However, the Sunderland crowd were disappointed by his absence although comforted by a rather one-sided 3-0 win. Whilst the absence of Kelso was significant there was some compensation in the form of Harry Jeffrey, who lined up for West End. Jeffrey would go on to represent not only West End and East End but Newcastle United.

By now both of Tyneside's major teams were having trouble attracting crowds to their grounds, although the arrival of Sunderland (who were nicknamed the Black Cats) at East End in November 1889 boosted the attendance to over 7,000, with a large contingent from Sunderland travelling to see their favourites. It was a productive short trip to Newcastle for the Black Cats, who ran out 4-0 winners.

Although the legend goes that Sunderland travelled to Tyneside in the 1880s and 1890s in a series of friendlies to assist in the financial well-being of their hosts there is no evidence that this was planned as such. It is true that Sunderland was a big draw on Tyneside and would undoubtedly have attracted a larger than normal audience for a football match, but any paternal influence on the part of the Wearsiders should not be inferred. There is irony, of course, in a notion that Sunderland helped to lay any solid monetary foundations for a Newcastle club. You'd be stretching credibility to the limit if you suggested that either club would play each other in the 21st century to save the skin of their rivals. This wouldn't happen, and neither team would ask for such help from the other.

By now Sunderland AFC were testing themselves more regularly against the best opposition that England and Scotland had to offer, and the game that probably clinched their admission into the Football League was the 7-2 demolition of the mighty Aston Villa at Newcastle Road on 5th April 1890. William McGregor, the acknowledged founder of the Football League, was astonished, saying that, in his opinion, Sunderland AFC "had a talented man in every position".

The legend of Sunderland AFC's "Team of all the Talents" was born and meant that the football club now merely had to submit an application for Football League membership to be accepted.

This duly occurred at a meeting of the Football League at the Douglas Hotel, Manchester, on 2nd May 1890, when Notts County, Burnley and Stoke applied for re-election; Darwen, Grimsby Town, Newton Heath, Sunderland and Sunderland Albion for election.

Sunderland's representatives at the meeting were James Marr and the Reverend Robinson Hindle of Eppleton Village. It's ironic that it was a member of the clergy, rather than a schoolteacher, who pleaded Sunderland's case; it was also backed by Alderman J P Hartley of Accrington.

No one could exclude Sunderland from league football on playing ability – the 1889/90 season had seen to that. The problem, however, was the travelling, as geographically Sunderland was out on a limb compared to the other clubs. Two things swung it; firstly all of the Football League sides had already visited Wearside, and, most importantly, the red and whites agreed to pay visiting teams' travelling expenses. This "guarantee" would last only one season and there is no evidence that any money was ever actually paid to a visiting team in recognition of this condition.

Sunderland was elected in place of Stoke City, and Wearside eagerly awaited the arrival of league football.

This decade was mainly about Sunderland, the senior and more successful northeast team at that point. Of the 22 cup and friendly games that the Wearside and Tyneside teams had played since the first encounter in 1881, Sunderland had lost just four, winning 13.

Sunderland was now a Football League club; Newcastle United would be, but not just yet. They had a couple of hurdles to overcome.

THE RISE OF NORTHEAST FOOTBALL

1890/91 to 1899/1900

It was hardly surprising that as a Football League club Sunderland met East End and West End only three times in total during the 1890/91 season.

On 29th November 1890 Glasgow Rangers should have been the visitors to Newcastle Road but a cup replay against Third Lanark meant that Sunderland had to hurriedly arrange a game with Newcastle West End. There was a time when a game between these sides would have been talked about for weeks before the match, but things had changed and the small attendance only confirmed the lack of interest there was in the game. The pitch had about an inch of snow covering it, as did the uncovered terraces, and the weather was cold and bright. Newcastle was thrashed 0-5, with Johnny Campbell scoring two for Sunderland.

Five months later the two clubs met again in a benefit game for West End's Barker, a stalwart of Tyneside football for more than a decade. The game at St James' Park was evenly contested, which was a credit to the Tyneside club who took the lead through Wood after 50 minutes, before Campbell – who else? – equalized two minutes later.

It was a cracking game of football from start to finish but regrettably only a restricted view was possible from the press box, making it impossible for the attending journalists to describe the action fully. This was due to West End allowing spectators to congregate in front of the press box, and when they stood on the benches provided rather than sitting on them reporters struggled to see large parts of the game.

On 30th April 1891 the football season was brought to a close in Newcastle when East End met Sunderland at Heaton. The weather was fine and a crowd of around 3,000 gathered as Sunderland took their position, attacking the railway goal. Mr William Turnbull, a local hotelier, kicked off, and in the opening minutes the ball moved rapidly from end to end. Sunderland emerged victorious 3-0. It was rather quaintly reported that:

After the match refreshments were served in Mr Turnbull's spacious Hotel adjoining the ground. Sunderland Chairman Mr Marr proposed a vote of thanks to Mr Turnbull for his hospitality and in doing so emphasised that Newcastle was a fine sporting town and would support good football. He considered there were a dozen clubs in Northumberland and Durham capable of forming a good league. Mr T Watson seconded the motion and it was carried with musical honours. Mr Turnbull replied.

Sunderland ended their first season in the Football League in seventh place, although this was not without controversy or difficulty for the Wearside club. Having lost their first two games against Burnley and Wolves they also had the indignity of a two-point deduction and a fine for fielding an ineligible player, Scottish goalkeeper Ted Doig, after a mix-up with his registration. Nevertheless, the club's performances had been satisfactory and it put into context the task that both East End and West End had in trying to defeat the Black Cats.

Matters were coming to a head on Tyneside during the 1891/92 season, and although five fixtures were played between Sunderland

and their Tyneside rivals, they were almost complete under the East End and West End banners. Indeed, the 8-1 thrashing of the latter on 2nd September 1891 was the last time the two teams would meet.

West End opened their season with this friendly at St James' Park after some extensive changes in the running of the club during the summer. Both the management and the constitution of the club had been changed after the previous unsuccessful club was wound up. Alterations to St James' Park during the close season meant that the enclosure now compared favourably with most in the country, although permission for the erection of a planned grandstand lay in the hands of the Town Improvement Committee of the Newcastle Corporation.

The Sunderland team arrived at 5pm and were put up at Mr Liddle's Clock Restaurant in Clayton Street, whilst the West End side changed at Mr J Black's Lord Hill Inn on Barrack Road. The weather was fine and a crowd of around 3,000 lined the barriers. Mr W Neasham was invited to start the game with a ball donated by Mr Liddle. West End won the toss and elected to play down the hill with a strong wind behind them.

Interestingly, the newly introduced system of having linesmen instead of umpires seemed to work well, as did the new penalty rule for penalizing handballs within 12 yards of the goal – none of the new penalty kicks were awarded, the deterrent value appeared to be enough.

The match was a rout, with Sunderland's Logan scoring five of the goals.

Although the Sunderland team and its supporters left West End for what would be the last time as opponents, the ever improving St James' Park would remain a monument for them for decades to come.

Five days later Sunderland travelled to Heaton to take on an

East team that had defeated the Casuals the week before; with the Black Cats having thrashed Wolves 5-2 at Newcastle Road in their last fixture a good game was in prospect and a crowd of around 3,000 had assembled. East End won the toss and once more the seemingly popular hotelier Mr W Turnbull kicked off for the visitors towards the Railway End.

Surprisingly, Sunderland lost 0-2 in their first loss against East End since their initial meeting way back in 1882. The visitors ended the game with 10 men when Smith received a "nasty kick"; however, with East End's Scott in "Stonewall Jackson" form in defence, 11 men for the visitors would have made no difference.

The cancellation of the Durham and Staffordshire county match on 26th September left Sunderland with a vacant date and, in order to fill a void, the return match with Newcastle East End was brought forward. This was deemed to demonstrate the sharp business acumen of the Sunderland committee as the unexpected defeat in Heaton three weeks previously had created quite a stir. It was hardly surprising therefore that a crowd of quite 5,000 people turned out for what was expected to be a keenly fought and attractive game.

The ground was in perfect condition if a little slippery in places and since East End's previous visit new accommodation had been built by Sunderland on the South side of the Newcastle Road ground. There was a great view of the playing area with a special private staircase for the despatch of messages to the Telegraph offices. The other stands were in perfect condition and even those who paid the smallest admission charge had a good view of the game.

From such media reports and the previous one at St James' Park we can glean that the advent of the Football League had intensified the more ambitious clubs' efforts to enhance the facilities at their stadiums.

The day was fine but a troublesome wind was blowing when East End won the toss, and they chose to play with it at their backs, attacking the Newcastle Road goal. Spence was injured and out of the East End side, which was a pity as he had done so well against Sunderland in Heaton. Wilson was dropped back to half-back by the home side and Miller played for the first time that season. Sunderland were due to play Aston Villa the following Monday and with this in mind they rested Porteous, Wilson and Campbell, although J Hannah returned to the forward line for the home side.

Although Sunderland were the Football League side, East End once more played well, to the extent that it was only the superior fitness, rather than ability of the home side, that proved the deciding factor, with the Black Cats' two goals coming in the last 20 minutes.

This was the Tyneside club's last ever trip to Sunderland AFC as Newcastle East End.

A meeting between East End and Sunderland took place on 9th January 1892. It was a magnificent game with Sunderland emerging victorious 6-4. However, the talking point wasn't the game but the blizzard conditions – the pitch was ankle-deep in snow.

Although there was a big crowd present – some 5,000 people turned up – there was little doubt that had the weather been fine the ground record could easily have been beaten. As we know, East End had beaten Sunderland earlier in the season, and, rather mischievously, there was a story going round on Wearside that East End were boasting that another defeat would be handed out when they next met. Sunderland had supposedly been instructed to play their hardest and to treat the game as if league points were at stake.

Although this had upped the ante, the East End committee were full of admiration for their Sunderland visitors, at that time probably the best team in England. East End expected to be beaten and any disappointment the home side felt stemmed from the fact that they failed to win after leading 4-1 at half-time. The snow was falling so heavily that the tramcar horses struggled to pull the Byker services, and with so much snow covering the ground many thought that the game would be called off.

However, it had been decided to give it a try although it was agreed to play only 35 minutes each way. Goodness knows what the score would have been had the teams played 90 minutes rather than 70!

It was three months later before the last meeting between East End and Sunderland that season; a match won by the visitors 4–1 at Heaton. In contrast to the previous game the sun was shining and there was a gentle breeze.

Newcastle United would commence battle with their soon to be bitter rivals as league champions as the 1891/92 season closed, with Sunderland remarkably heading the table – so much, so soon for the Wearside club. Unbeaten at home with 13 straight victories at Newcastle Road they had scored 93 goals home and away with a goal difference of plus 57. Five points ahead of Preston North End in second place, the club ended the season with 13 friendlies and won them all!

Prior to the start of the 1892/93 season East End tried to gain admittance to the First Division of the Football League, at a meeting ironically held in Sunderland. Although not successful in that bid they were admitted to the Second Division, but due to the standard of the opposition they would face East End rejected the opportunity. Their thinking was simple – teams such as Ardwick and Darwen were no better than those they were already facing.

Therefore East End's first game at St James' Park took place on 3rd September 1892, a friendly match against the Glasgow giants from Celtic. Although the Scots won the match 1-0 the crowd of 6,000 was larger than normal. When Celtic moved on to play Sunderland on Wearside two days later, they lost the game to a solitary Johnny Campbell goal.

On 7th September 1892 East End played the then league champions, Sunderland, for the very last time before they changed their name. Fittingly the match ended all square, 2-2, with Tom Crate giving the Tynesiders an early lead, which was soon cancelled out by David Hannah. East End regained the lead through Wallace after 23 minutes but the Wearsiders struck back just five minutes later when Gillespie scored a lovely goal from a mazy run and low shot, giving the home custodian David Whitton no chance to block it. Interestingly, this now meant that East End had lost only one of the previous six meetings with their Wearside rivals, and the media reported that the home side were playing splendidly and each pass was greeted with cheers from the crowd.

After 28 matches against both East End and West End, spanning nearly 11 years, Sunderland AFC were about to formally play the club that would rise to become their nemesis: Newcastle United.

The name change came about as a result of continuing fan apathy (as far as the East End committee was concerned) on Tyneside, and at a meeting at Bath Lane Hall (Bath Lane would become infamous in the 1970s due to a mass fight between NUFC and SAFC fans prior to one of the derby games) near to St James' Park on Friday 9th December 1892 it was unanimously decided to change the club's name to Newcastle United in an effort to appeal to the whole city rather than the parochial area where the club had its original roots.

Although not significant at the time, with hindsight it can be looked upon as bizarre that Newcastle United retained their all-red or red-and-white striped shirts for the time being; the colours, of course, of Sunderland AFC! The world famous black-and-white stripes would not be seen until 1894.

For the record Newcastle United's first ever match was at home to fellow northeasterners Middlesbrough; the Geordies winning 2-1.

However, it was not without controversy, with the Newcastle side being accused of taking it easy after the interval due to bribes that had been paid to them by some of the less principled members of the Teesside support. Amazingly the allegations were to all intents and purposes upheld as a series of suspensions and sackings took place at St James'.

With such matters forgotten about, United's first ever game with Sunderland took place on 25th February 1893, and confidence was running high that they could give their Wearside rivals a good game. However, the home side were swept aside in front of their own partisan crowd to the tune of 1-6, with the Black Cats taking the lead in the very first minute through David Hannah. It went downhill from there.

Indeed the next 14 friendly and testimonial games between the two sides resulted in a solitary win for United, who conceded a mammoth 39 goals during the process! Of the next 24 games that the two teams would play against each other in what remained of the decade only five were played on Wearside, and in what would become a regular feature for Sunderland fans the Wearsiders won only once at home against their Tyneside rivals. United, by and large, have historically travelled well to Sunderland territory, particularly recently where they have lost just once since 1979/80.

The United players in those Victorian times were interesting characters as the club's official historian Paul Joannou recalls:

Crielly like McKane was suspended for bad language, Jeffrey was told not to attend the club for two weeks because he was a "non trier" while McKane found himself in trouble again when for the last league game of the (1892/93) season at Middlesbrough, he failed to turn up! There were many other incidents of lax training and frequent reprimands were issued.

By 1893 Newcastle were desperate to gain entry into the Football League and once more attempted to go directly into the First Division. Although they were again refused they were given the opportunity to become a member of the Second Division. This time they accepted the invitation, although the fact that Liverpool, Middlesbrough Ironopolis and Arsenal were also elected probably helped their decision.

Sunderland were, of course, playing in the First Division and, indeed, had won the League Championship for a second time in 1892/93, winning the title by a massive 11-point margin from Preston North End and, in doing so, becoming the first team to score 100 league goals in a season. Therefore competitive league fixtures did not occur between the two sides until 1898/99, following Newcastle United's first promotion at the end of their 1897/98 league campaign as runners-up to Second Division champions Burnley.

United had to wait until 21st April 1894 to record their first win against Sunderland, a friendly at St James' Park in which they ran out 4-1 winners. Whilst not detracting from the victory, the Wearsiders had just returned to the northeast from Scotland where they had played a gruelling eight games in just 14 days. The visitors therefore rested four players for the game and played Hugh Wilson out of position at full-back rather than his usual half-back position. Nevertheless the home side thoroughly deserved their win and by the end had their rivals demoralized.

Sunderland travelled to St James' Park once more just nine days later and won 3-1, although the significance of the match is not in the scoreline but the fact that it was the last time that the two teams would play each other with the United kit as red and white. At a board meeting on 2nd August 1894 it was agreed to change the official colours to black and white, although this was not in deference to their rivals playing in red and white but due to increasing colour clashes with league opponents. It should be noted that at that time football clubs did not have multiple strips and had to improvise at times to avoid kit clashes with the opposition. Therefore the 5th September 1894 match between Sunderland and Newcastle was the first where the home side officially played in black-and-white striped kit. It didn't help United as they promptly lost 1-4.

What is interesting is that, a bit like Sunderland choosing red and white (mooted to be taken from the Washington coat of arms) over their original all-blue kit, there is no definitive reason why United chose black and white. Several theories were put forward but never proven.

Sunderland won the league title for a third time in 1894/95, this time by five points from Everton, who were in second place. Newcastle ended 10th in the second tier, that division being sewn up by Bury, who won it by nine points from Notts County.

On 23rd September 1896 the first testimonial match between United and Sunderland took place to the benefit of ace marksman Johnny Campbell – then with the Black Cats – at Newcastle Road. It was estimated that the game raised about £65 for Campbell and the crowd was boosted by a contingent from Newcastle who arrived by tram. The visitors opened the scoring through Wardrope and it was left to a last-gasp equalizer by Wilson to salvage some pride for the home side.

By now the Tyne–Wear games were attracting massive crowds in excess of 15,000 and the first league meeting of the two sides took place on 24th December 1898 at Roker Park (Sunderland had moved to their famous arena earlier that year, playing their first competitive fixture against Liverpool on 10th September 1898). Newcastle were the ninth team to visit Roker and if it hadn't been for Burnley winning there two weeks previously (Burnley were also the first team to defeat Sunderland in Football League competition in September 1890 at Newcastle Road) the Tynesiders would have had the distinction of becoming the first team to defeat Sunderland at the new ground; they consoled themselves in being the second team to achieve this feat following a 3-2 victory. As newspaper reports of the day testified, this was a momentous day:

The first ever league meeting between Newcastle and Sunderland attracted widespread interest with Sunderland starting slight favourites in the light of their better performances this season. It was estimated that at least 8,000 enthusiasts joined trains at Newcastle Central Station and numerous private brakes and charabancs augmented this total. Despite 18 special trains being laid on the railway company failed completely to cope with the numbers of people clamouring for speedy conveyance to Sunderland.

The average number crammed into each compartment was 18 to 20 and on the return journey the trains were even more crowded. Such miserable accommodation is unfair on the travelling public and is poor testimony to the organising ability of the Railway staff. A further cause for complaint was the increased tariff charged for admission by the Sunderland directors. However the tremendous enthusiasm for the game outweighed all other considerations and with a crowd of fully 30,000 Sunderland's coffers will have increased by about £800.

The Newcastle team did not arrive until 1-30pm having taken nearly an hour and twenty minutes to make a journey of only 12 miles.

Sunderland went ahead through Leslie, the man who had scored the Black Cats' first ever goal at Roker Park, but Wardrope equalized. Peddie then scored two to give the away side a priceless lead, and although Leslie later notched his second of the match Newcastle held on to win.

The two teams arranged a Shrove Tuesday friendly match at Roker Park on 14th February 1899 and if Sunderland thought that revenge would be sweet following their Christmas Eve defeat they were in for a shock. The visitors were in no mood to oblige and surprised the Black Cats by winning once more, this time 4-3. Again it was Peddie who proved to be a thorn in the side of the red and whites, as he scored the winner in the very last minute.

Ironically, the next two league fixtures between the sides were played at St James' Park and Sunderland emerged victorious in both to even the score up.

The 22nd April 1899 fixture witnessed, predictably, a massive crowd of 25,000, which filled St James' Park to capacity. Much to the despair of the Newcastle United committee some 500 people had to be turned away from the entrance, although they consoled themselves by hunting out every conceivable vantage point outside the ground, including crowded balconies on the houses on Leazes Terrace. The only goal of the game was scored by Sunderland's McLatchie, to which *the Wearside contingent in the crowd went wild with delight*.

For the 23rd December 1899 visit to Tyneside Sunderland made two changes, with Billy Hogg replacing Crawford, who had been injured in the previous week's Roker Park draw against Sheffield United, and Beckton coming in for Farquhar. Newcastle made only one change, with Lindsay coming in for Birnie. The crowd was around 21,000, which was down on the pre-match estimates, however, the lack of a full railway service and an early kick-off contributed to this. In a nod to the season, there was a three-inch carpet of snow on the pitch, which left it slippery.

Sunderland's 4-2 win was as remarkable as the home side's collapse, as a 1-2 half-time deficit was overturned spectacularly with three goals in 16 second-half minutes from the visitors. The man of the moment as far as the Black Cats were concerned was their Whitburn-born forward Bobby Hogg, who notched a hat-trick – the first man to achieve such a feat in the history of competitive games between the two sides.

The 19th century was drawing to a close and it ended football-wise for Tyne and Wear on 28th April 1900, when Newcastle United once more defeated Sunderland at Roker Park, this time 2-1, in the last league game of the season. Fraser and Gardner gave the visitors a deserved two-goal lead in what was a desultory affair, although Fulton pulled one back for Sunderland just before the interval. Perhaps the most exciting moment in the game was when a stray dog ran on to the pitch in the second half!

The 1899/1900 season ended with Sunderland claiming third place in the First Division, well adrift of title winners Aston Villa, whilst Newcastle achieved their best league position to date: fifth, five points behind Sunderland.

As far as football was concerned the 19th century had now ended for the two northeast giants – a lot had been achieved, but so much more lay in store.

NUFC DOMINATE DESPITE HUMILIATION

1900/01 to 1909/10

If the 19th century had been characterized by a plethora of friendly matches between Newcastle and Sunderland such fixtures would start to reduce as competitive football took over. To prove this there were only four non-competitive fixtures played between the first teams in the entire decade. The crowds attracted to the games grew larger, the matches took on more significance and, as a result, the behaviour of the spectators would worsen, with some explosive pitch invasions, stabbings and general criminality.

However, there was also some classic football matches played, some wonderful footballers on view, and we shall explore more legendary characters from both sides.

The decade commenced with perhaps its best match, a 1-1 draw at Roker Park. The game was more akin to a cup tie than a league fixture, and almost 30,000 crammed into the ground in what was an eagerly anticipated contest between two teams who were unbeaten so far that season. One look at the line-ups, as follows, indicated that they were filled with high-quality men; this would be borne out with four league titles, one runners-up title, and four third-placed finishes between the two teams during the 1900 to 1910 period:

Sunderland: *Doig, McCombie, Watson, Ferguson, McAllister, Farquhar, Hogg (W), Common, Millar, Livingstone, McLatchie.*

Newcastle United: *Kingsley, Burgess, Gardner (D), Ghee, Aitken, Carr, Niblo, Gardner (A), Peddie, McFarlane, Fraser.*

The visitors' goal was scored by Andrew McCombie, an own goal just two minutes before the interval as he tried to clear an effort by Gardner but merely helped it into the net. The Scotsman would go on to play for the Magpies, leaving Sunderland in acrimonious circumstances in an incident that rocked the Black Cats. He also had an occupation outside of football, that of a pianoforte tuner, something that would lead to trouble.

Sunderland's goal was scored by the much vaunted George Livingstone after an hour. The Scotsman, a teetotaller recently arrived from Heart of Midlothian, notched his third goal in just six games since his arrival from the Edinburgh club, although he wouldn't last long on Wearside and moved north of the border to Glasgow Celtic, having played a mere 30 games for the red and whites.

The intensity of the burgeoning rivalry between Sunderland and Newcastle United was emphasized on the return Good Friday league fixture scheduled for 5th April 1901. It was estimated that anywhere up to 70,000 people descended on St James' Park; the stadium at the time held barely 30,000. The ensuing chaos resulted in thousands of people spilling on to the pitch, and the main stand structure was under severe pressure – there was even the possibility that it could collapse. Play was impossible, despite both teams taking to the field, and when it was announced that the referee had abandoned the game all hell broke loose. The fans, at first good-natured, turned ugly and charged the police, who had to use batons to curb the civil disorder, and it wasn't until two hours after the scheduled 5pm kick-off that the ground was cleared. Furthermore, during the chaos an unlucky fan fell off the roof of the main stand (where he had climbed up for a better view). As a result of the disorder an FA commission was set up that effectively exonerated Newcastle from any blame, although insufficient fencing and policing were blamed for much of what had transpired.

The rearranged fixture was set for 24th April 1901, and by this time Newcastle's faint title hopes had ended: they lay seventh. Sunderland, by comparison, were top of the table, and the resulting 2-0 win for the Wearsiders, with both goals scored by the Hoggs, kept them top (they would subsequently surrender the championship to Liverpool by a mere two points). However, the main concern was that the game should pass off without spectator incident and, with a bigger police presence in and around St James' Park, order was maintained, with the crowd kept to below 20,000. Kick-off wasn't until 5.45pm, which gave factory workers, such as those from the Elswick Ordnance Works and others, an opportunity to attend the game, arriving straight from work in their overalls and with blackened faces. United's portion of the gate receipts, given as around £650, was shared amongst local charities as a gesture of goodwill following on from the previous Good Friday debacle.

Again, nothing was left to chance in the first Tyne–Wear encounter of the 1901/02 season at St James' Park: some 60 police officers were on duty, supplemented by six mounted policemen. Yet the attendance of 23,330 was disappointing; however, this was a reflection on the fact that the turnstiles opened at 1pm and shut promptly at 2.30pm, with many fans being turned away. Sunderland won the game 1-0 with a first-half goal from Gemmell, a shot from 30 yards that seemed to be going nowhere but curled viciously into the net. Nevertheless, long before the end the Newcastle fans were streaming out of the ground, abandoning what was a fairly uneventful encounter. The amazing statistic to emerge from the match was that in the seven league games played between the sides since Newcastle's promotion the home side had yet to win. The Geordie frustration was summed up by one media report which stated that:

Combination (play) was totally absent and individual effort and shooting rare. Niblo seemed overwhelmed by the occasion and his play was wild and erratic.

Just one month later Newcastle United registered the division's highest league victory that season, thrashing Notts County 8-0!

A first competitive Tyne–Wear home win was registered by Newcastle United in the FA Cup second-round game at St James' Park in February 1902 with a Ronald Orr goal just two minutes from time, settling a good match. The game took place midweek as the original Saturday game had been called off due to heavy snowfall in the northeast. Even when it did get the go-ahead severe frost meant that there were still a couple of inches of snow on and around the pitch. A curious incident occurred towards the end of the first half when the original match ball was kicked out of the stadium, lost, and a new ball had to be found to recommence the game. Following Orr's goal it was reported that:

Hats, caps, sticks and everything else went up into the air as the crowd realized that the game was won and lost.

It was a fair result, as Newcastle had obviously been the better side, with the Sunderland goal having had *"many miraculous escapes"*.

Newcastle progressed to the quarter-finals where they were knocked out by the eventual cup winners of 1902, Sheffield United, who featured the ex-Sunderland player Alf Common, famously the first player ever transferred for a four-figure sum. In fact Common scored in the final at the Crystal Palace against Southampton, a match that was replayed after that initial 1-1 draw.

On Easter Monday 1902 Sunderland again tried but failed to defeat their Tyneside rivals at Roker Park, although the 0-0 draw was anything but dull. In fact, in an exciting game the Black Cats had a remarkable let-off when McColl, with only Doig in the Sunderland goal to beat, struck the goalkeeper with his shot and somehow the ball bounced out to safety. However, at the other end Kingsley turned in a man-of-the-match performance for United with four outstanding saves from the home forwards.

The media reports made for interesting reading, giving the backdrop to the fixture:

Sunderland returned from Seaton Carew on the morning of the match and the team was selected at midday. Both Gemmell and McLatchie were unable to play through injury. Newcastle were unchanged. The team drove over to Sunderland in a brake to avoid the extraordinary volume of traffic on the railways. An enormous number of Newcastle fans wanted to travel with hundreds being left on the platform after each Sunderland bound train left. The weather could not have been better apart from a strongish breeze.

Half an hour before the kick off Roker Park looked full but crowds of people were still streaming in through the gates and with 15 minutes to go until the start about 28,000 people would be in the enclosure. Sunderland wore white shirts to avoid a clash with Newcastle's stripes. Newcastle won the toss and elected to play with the wind and sun at their backs.

In all some 34,819 watched the game, the highest number to date for a Tyne–Wear derby game, although that figure would be made to look paltry just three years later at St James' Park when the first 50,000-plus crowd would congregate.

The 1901/02 season ended with Sunderland winning their fourth First Division title, and Everton in second place. Although there was obvious joy on Wearside it was tempered in June 1902 when their captain, Matthew Ferguson, died of pleuro-pneumonia at the age of 26. He was born in Bellshill, a suburb of Glasgow, and signed for Sunderland in 1896 from Mossend. In his sixth and final season on Wearside he had been a mainstay in winning the championship. The fans were devastated.

The first derby game of the 1902/03 season took place two days after Christmas at Roker Park, and once more the home side failed to defeat their Tyneside rivals on Wearside, as an exciting game, watched by an estimated 27,000, ended 0-0.

After the match at Blackburn on Christmas Day Sunderland stayed overnight in Leeds and travelled to Seaton Carew on the Friday morning, where they remained overnight. At 11am on the Saturday they returned to Sunderland and had lunch at the town's Queens Hotel. The directors didn't choose the team until an hour before the kick-off. The Newcastle directors also had selection problems. Their sick list was long and it was impossible for them to put their best team out; consequently Caie who had been selected at centre-forward had to go to half-back, with Gardner occupying the centre-forward spot. McColl had been injured in a previous game against Hibernian and Roberts was suffering from jaundice so reserve half-back Birnie was played at outside-left. Rutherford went inside and Stonehouse was played on the right wing with Veitch as his partner.

Rutherford was known as "the Newcastle Flier" and came from Percy Main. He had 11 brothers and sisters. Solid as a rock for Newcastle, the winger scored 93 league and cup goals for the Magpies.

However, in truth the forward line looked all over the place and it was quite experimental. The Newcastle team had travelled to Wearside in a brake. About 4,000 supporters travelled from Newcastle and they were better accommodated by the local railway company than on several previous occasions. The official attendance was given as 25,000 although this didn't include the 2,000 season ticket holders. In total the gate receipts amounted to £850.

The weather was excellent and consequently the gates were opened at 12pm but the crowd came into Roker Park slowly. In fact at 1.30pm there were only about 6,000 inside the ground. When the home side emerged it was reported that they were "*wearing new shirts for the occasion*", presumably red and white!

The travelling Newcastle fans were delighted with what they saw from their patched-up team and it was reported that:

[the] understudies however played better than the men they replaced and Gardner at centre forward dribbled and handled his wings with much success though he might have tried a few more shots. Stonehouse and Birnie were quick as well as tricky but the honours in attack went to Rutherford.

A rare friendly between the two sides took place in February 1903 and although it was poorly attended Newcastle had the satisfaction of defeating Sunderland on home soil.

However, with Sunderland closing in on another league title it was a game against their nearest rivals for the league, the Wednesday (who would become Sheffield Wednesday), the following month that looked crucial. Denying Sunderland what looked like three perfectly legitimate goals, the referee, Mr Armitt of Leek, made himself unpopular, particularly when the home side lost the game 0-1, dealing the Black Cats a blow in their bid for a fifth league crown. The Wearside crowd took defeat badly and they not only assaulted the referee after the game but also stoned the Sheffield players' transport in Roker Baths Road. For this the Football League executive ordered Sunderland to play their next "home" fixture away from Roker. Sensing a golden financial opportunity the Newcastle directors offered their Wearside neighbours the use of St James' Park, an offer which was gratefully accepted by their red-and-white counterparts. That "home" game would be against near neighbours Middlesbrough (approximately 25 to 30 miles from Sunderland and the Wearsiders' nearest rivals, geographically, after Newcastle United). As if that wasn't ironic enough Sunderland also had to face Newcastle in their final league game of the season at St James'!

The equation could hardly have been starker for the Wearsiders: win both games at St James' and the title would likely be theirs, fail to win one of the fixtures and their ambitions were over.

The first part of that equation was successfully negotiated when, on 18th April, goals from Hewitt and Millar assisted Sunderland to a 2-1 win, although a late strike by the Boro's Robertson seven minutes from time left the Sunderland fans amongst the mammoth 26,000 crowd anxious.

Interestingly, the newspaper reports of the day state that *"rousing cheers"* greeted Hewitt's goal for Sunderland so we can assume from that that there was not only a large contingent of Sunderland fans at St James' Park (their largest ever following on Tyneside?) but that many Newcastle fans may well have turned up to cheer on Sunderland. This would bear out tales that up until the 1960s many fans watched both clubs' home games on alternate weeks.

On 25th April 1903, the last scheduled game of the 1902/03 Football League season, it came down to this: a Sunderland win would almost certainly mean that the Black Cats would be league champions, defeat by their Tyneside rivals would probably cost them the ultimate prize.

Bizarrely (well, certainly bizarre in the current climate between the two clubs), Football League representatives turned up at St

James' as a reminder to the Tyneside club to try hard and not allow their Wearside neighbours to win (as if!), although with Sunderland having won all four of their previous league encounters at Newcastle, the administrators perhaps had a point.

In front of league representatives (and 500 supporters from Sheffield) Sunderland were confident of victory; however, in what turned out to be a crushing blow for the Wearsiders in front of a huge 26,562 crowd Bob McCall scored for United after 47 minutes to inflict perhaps the biggest blow ever in the history of Tyne–Wear derby games. Sunderland's league-title ambitions lay in tatters.

In the drama the fact that Newcastle had also won their first home league game against Sunderland and in doing so created a Tyne–Wear derby record of four consecutive clean sheets – which included one in the FA Cup – that stands to this day, was lost.

Not only did Sunderland surrender the league title to Wednesday, who pipped them by a solitary point, the Wearsiders ended up third when Aston Villa won five matches in the last 15 days of the season, scoring 15 goals in the process.

Perhaps the most important early development in the 1903/04 season was the completion of the new Ayresome Park stadium in Middlesbrough. The Teessiders' first visitors were Glasgow Celtic, who dealt them a 0-1 defeat. Later, Sunderland became the first of the northeast teams to play Middlesbrough at their new home on 12th September 1903, when they inflicted a first home defeat on the Boro 2-3. Like so many of the stadiums at that time Ayresome Park was built by the Scottish architect Archibald Leitch, a fan of Glasgow Rangers, whose CV included construction work at both Roker Park and St James' Park.

The first Tyne–Wear derby game of the season took place on Boxing Day, with Sunderland at a slight advantage due to six days off since their last game on 19th December against Sheffield United. Newcastle United had played the Blades on Christmas Day – a 2-2 draw – at Bramall Lane, travelling back overnight.

Sunderland fielded a full-strength team, having enjoyed their festive break at Seaton Carew (a seaside town near Hartlepool), whilst United had injury worries with Howie ruled out; his place was taken by Turner who filled the right-wing berth, partnering Rutherford up front.

Sunderland were conspicuously represented by battalions of supporters and 30 minutes before the start all areas of St James Park were crowded. Altogether 28,797 people paid for admission and the total attendance with ticket holders was estimated at 30,000 with receipts of about £900.

Consternation was raised by both clubs when the referee, Mr Lewis from Blackburn, missed his train connection; however, the game was not delayed as both clubs agreed that one of the linesmen, Mr Dennis of Middlesbrough, should take charge until the arrival of Mr Lewis, 20 minutes late. Appleyard kicked off for Newcastle towards the town goal and against a stiff breeze.

Sunderland started off as much the better team and the home goal was under siege with a lucky escape for the Tynesiders after just 10 minutes. However, after 20 minutes Arthur Bridgett opened the scoring for the visitors following good work from Buckle and Gemmell. Willis, in trying to clear, merely knocked the ball into the path of the Sunderland striker and he made no mistake from close range. Barely three minutes later Bridgett, in acres of space, made it 0-2. If Sunderland thought that Newcastle were down and out they were mistaken, as with just three minutes remaining Rutherford reduced the arrears and the excitement reached fever pitch in what was described as a good-natured crowd. However, the pendulum swung back in the Black Cats' favour when Buckle scored a third for the visitors with 30 seconds remaining, as the home side charged upfield in search of an equalizer.

The Geordies wouldn't have to wait long to exact revenge, as on New Year's Day 1904 the two teams met again at Roker Park. The crowd was huge at around 37,000 (a record attendance at the time), and the first set of fans had been travelling by train from all outposts of the northeast from as early as 10am that morning. However, once again the local train companies were found wanting and had real trouble coping with the influx of passengers, particularly on arrival at Monkwearmouth railway station (which was about one mile from Roker Park).

Newcastle were refreshed, and *"having regained their full vitality and virility amidst the salubrious and breezy atmosphere of their special training quarters at Alnmouth they met Sunderland on equal terms and this battle between the giants was fought with grim determination"*. Newcastle were much the better side for the entire match but despite their skill and endeavour the opening 45 minutes ended goalless. However, that would not remain the case for long and within five minutes of the resumption of play the visitors were level when Orr scored following a goalmouth *"scrimmage"*.

Nevertheless, the luck on the day was with Sunderland, and try as they might for a second goal it just wouldn't come for United and they fell for a sucker punch with just six minutes remaining when the home side were awarded a dubious penalty, scored by McCombie. A newspaper report of the day interestingly reported the incident thus,

The referee awarded a penalty kick for a foul charge on McAllister. Not one spectator in a thousand expected this but Mr Lewis insisted that Aitken had impeded McAllister with his hands. Aitken emphatically protested against this sensational and disastrous ruling and denied the foul claiming that McAllister had run full tilt into him with his head down. McColl suggested that Mr Lewis would have difficulty in explaining the decision and it was peculiar that the linesmen when interviewed "did not see the incident".

One hundred years later managers are the ones who remarkably comment that they "did not see the incident" (I can think of one in particular who never appears to see anything against his side whatever the misdemeanour), and it would have been good to record what McColl actually said to the referee – I doubt it was repeatable!

Newcastle United left Wearside feeling aggrieved and if reports are to be believed this feeling was not without foundation.

This game was to be one of Andrew McCombie's last for Sunderland AFC and, remarkably, he would be a Newcastle United player within weeks. What became known as "the McCombie Affair" had untold ramifications for both northeast clubs.

The issue started in the close season of 1903/04 when Sunderland AFC gave McCombie £100 to enable him to start up a piano business. It was given on the understanding that on receiving a benefit game he would repay the money. The benefit game was duly designated to be the Football League encounter with Middlesbrough on 9th January 1904, a match that drew a sizeable 15,000 crowd. However, when the club approached McCombie about repaying the "loan" he refused, insisting that the money had been a gift. The money he received for his benefit game looked to be considerable as the press reported that *"if it is true that McCombie received the money paid for tickets he must have received pretty near the whole gate for the spectators were well canvassed by Macs friends both in the main thoroughfare and at the entrances to the ground".* The issue simmered at Roker Park and although McCombie travelled to Anfield and played in the next home game against Bury, he was absent for the game at Blackburn on 30th January 1904, not only refusing to play again for Sunderland but even refusing to train at Seaton Carew in advance of the trip to Lancashire.

By now the whole affair was spreading discontent within the Sunderland ranks and, furthermore, McCombie was unhappy with his salary. He then refused to travel to Manchester City and in fact he was not even in the party which trained at Seaton Carew prior to the game.

He would never play for Sunderland again.

The spat between club and player had entered the public arena and a clamour for McCombie's signature began, with clubs such as Rangers and Celtic as well as Aston Villa chasing him. However, the Scotsman decided to stay in the northeast and in February 1904 he signed for Newcastle United in a deal thought to be worth around £700.

At the time McCombie was perhaps the best full-back in the United Kingdom; to put his influence into perspective, in his first full season with the Magpies they won the Football League for the first time.

However, the matter didn't end with his transfer. The Football Association opened up an enquiry into the £100 "gift" and ordered Sunderland to take legal action against McCombie. A court of law judged that the money constituted a loan, which the Scotsman ultimately ended up repaying. The FA took exception to this ruling and insisted that Sunderland AFC had violated the games rules. The club's books were deemed as not showing a true record of its financial affairs.

The upshot was that Sunderland AFC were fined £250, six directors were suspended for two and a half years, Alex Watson (financial secretary) for 18 months and Alex Mackie (manager/secretary) for three months.

This came as a huge blow to the club, and it was even mooted that they may have to be wound up. J P Henderson vacated the chair to Sinclair Todd in September 1904 although Fred Taylor, who had first appeared on the SAFC board of directors in 1896, remained.

Mackie would leave the club in the 1904/05 close season for Middlesbrough and be replaced by Bob Kyle from Belfast Distillery; the McCombie Affair was thought to be a reason for his departure.

Although the Tyne–Wear League derby games would not be seen again until September, April saw Newcastle visit Roker Park to play a testimonial game for the Black Cat stalwart Jimmy Millar. Sunderland won the game 3-0, shattering NUFC's previously great record at Roker, but it was sad for Millar that only 3,000 were at the ground to witness the affair. He deserved better than that having served the red and whites twice over a 14-year period, making 260 appearances and scoring 122 goals. Interestingly, in this game McCombie played for the Magpies.

The 1903/04 season ended with Newcastle United in fourth place with Sunderland sixth.

The rest of the decade was all about the Magpies, although the Black Cats would have one brief moment in the sun against them.

In September 1904 Sunderland travelled to St James' Park to play in a match for the benefit of the officers and men of the fleet. Patriotic Tynesiders and Wearsiders turned out in force, with the attendance given as 20,000.

The directors had brightened up the ground with bunting and the principal stand was daintily picked out with bright ensigns. The bottom half of the stand was reserved for men of the Fleet with the bulk of them wearing their bright straw hats. Their Lordships kicked off at 3-25 with Sunderland playing uphill.

"Their Lordships" was in reference to the then Admiral of the Fleet, Lord Beresford, who had also served as a member of parliament, representing County Waterford until 1880.

Sunderland took the lead with a fine Bridgett goal, as he took a superb pass from Common in his stride and smashed it past Watts.

In what was an always entertaining game Sunderland's Buckle dislocated his arm, had to be attended by the Newcastle doctor in attendance Dr Farquharson, and left the field immediately for the dressing room. Newcastle equalized through a 20-yard thunderbolt from Appleyard that beat the Sunderland custodian, Rowlandson, all ends up. Sunderland's winner was scored in the second half by Gemmell, although Watts, in a despairing dive, almost got to the ball.

The first competitive encounter between the two sides took place on Christmas Eve 1904 at Roker Park on a pitch that was treacherous underfoot. As a result the game suffered, although the home side had the upper hand throughout, a factor perhaps being the rubber studs that the Sunderland team had chosen to nail into their boots. In fact the match couldn't have got off to a worse start for the visitors as they fell behind in the very first minute to a goal from Jackson. What decided the game was a three-minute spell inside the first half when, on 29 minutes, McWilliam scored a soft goal for Newcastle, with Webb in the home goal totally deceived. Sunderland went back in front within 60 seconds when a Hogg shot was beaten out by Lawrence, the Magpie custodian, only for Buckle to follow up and tap the rebound home in what was his first game since he dislocated his arm in the Channel Fleet friendly. However, had Watson not treated young Rutherford in a most unsportsmanlike way Newcastle would have had an equalizer before the interval. Rutherford had the full-back well beaten as he moved into the penalty area only to have his legs swept from under him. There was no hesitation from Mr Kirkham the referee in the award of a penalty kick but it would have been better if McCombie or Veitch had taken it instead of Appleyard. The pressure on both Webb and Appleyard must have been intense during the long delay while the referee made sure the players were in the correct position before the kick was taken. Attempting to put the ball past Webb's left hand, Appleyard sent it a couple of yards wide.

Jackson scored the winner for Sunderland on the hour mark with a clever shot over the heads of several players but in the end it was reported that Newcastle had tried to play *"too scientifically"* in the mud, and with the Black Cats subsequently mastering the conditions better, the Magpies sealed their own fate.

One bright note for Newcastle had been the way in which, for once, the local rail company had coped with the estimated 7,000 supporters who had left Central station in the hours leading up to the game. With a mere 20 spectators in average to any one carriage, some 350 of them were well organized on this occasion.

Remarkably this was Sunderland AFC's very first competitive victory over Newcastle on home soil.

In the dying embers of the 1904/05 season, and with Newcastle going for the title, a 1-3 defeat at home by Sunderland on 22nd April 1905 could have been fatal to the Magpie title hopes but, as it was, Everton, the league leaders, lost at Woolwich Arsenal to leave the race wide open. You could say it was a case of déjà vu, given the events of a couple of seasons before when this fixture and a subsequent Newcastle win denied the Black Cats the League Championship.

As, in the previous week, Newcastle had succumbed 0-2 to Aston Villa in the FA Cup final at the Crystal Palace, this wasn't the time to hit bad form. That match had been watched by 101,117, the second highest FA Cup final crowd ever at that time, with two goals by Hampton sealing the Magpies' fate.

As can be imagined, back on Tyneside the game against their Wearside rivals was the match that everyone wanted to see. If Newcastle had won, they could have effectively claimed the title for the first time on home soil. As it was, it was wins at Sheffield Wednesday and Middlesbrough over the course of the next seven days that saw them clinch it.

Another huge police presence was on duty and, while the gates closed at 2pm with approaching 30,000 inside the stadium, another 2,000 scaled the walls to gain admittance. There was at least another 15,000 to 25,000 locked out.

Sunderland won the game in an explosive six-minute spell when first George Holley and then the Belfast-born Harold Buckle scored. Veitch reduced the arrears with a penalty but Holley again, after 83 minutes, (dubiously) beat the offside trap, closed in on goal and slipped the ball past Lawrence.

It was hard lines on the home side that they lost Gardner within half an hour of the start and ended up playing with 10 men, as the Newcastle defender had effectively shackled Buckle up until his incapacitation.

This was Sunderland's first ever league double over Newcastle.

Nevertheless, Newcastle could console themselves with their first League Championship, sewn up on Teesside, just a few days later – and, with an FA Cup final appearance to reflect on, it had been an excellent season for the Magpies.

Sunderland were about to go through a period of transition but would emerge with a fine side, come the early 1910s, under Bob Kyle, a man who would turn out to be the club's longest serving manager.

The 1905/06 season was the 35th competitive English Football League campaign and although the First Division would be won by Liverpool the Magpies ended a creditable fourth. Sunderland by contrast would end up 14th, their second lowest league position ever after the 15th place in 1896/97. Indeed it was a baptism of fire for new manager Bob Kyle, and he would have two more poor seasons (by Sunderland AFC standards) before he created his best team, which included the near double-winning side of 1912/13.

As luck would have it the Magpies faced the Black Cats at Roker Park on the very first day of the new season, 2nd September 1905

– and what a brilliant game it was. Although Sunderland deservedly won 3-2 there was much to admire in both sides including the goalkeeping brilliance of Lawrence in the visiting goal. It is worth mentioning at this point that Lawrence has the penalty record in Tyne–Wear derby history, having saved four in all. The only spot kick to beat him was Jackie Mordue's in 1913.

The crowd was estimated at 30,000 although match reports indicated that this was likely to have been an underestimate as fans travelled from far and wide to take in the spectacle. Once more the railways were put to the test as some 70 per cent of those attending travelled by that means to Sunderland, including an estimated 6,000 from Newcastle Central station.

There was an interesting addition to the Newcastle United squad for the game. Wally Hardinge had been signed in the close season after some good performances in the Kent Football League. Hardinge played cricket for Kent, becoming one of the most prolific batsmen in English county history, scoring over 33,000 first-class runs, including 75 centuries, although his England appearances were limited, which was hardly surprising as the men keeping him out of the Test arena were none other than (Sir) Jack Hobbs and Herbert Sutcliffe, two of the greatest batsmen of any era, never mind this one. For Hardinge though this wouldn't be a good day as he looked to be on a different wavelength from his team-mates, particularly the wingers, and the 1915 Wisden Cricketer of the Year would make few appearances on Tyneside before being transferred to Sheffield United.

McCombie, recently signed from Sunderland, was in the Newcastle ranks but there was nothing he could do to stop a lovely low shot from the home side's Arthur Bridgett careering past Lawrence in the visiting goal after just three minutes.

Newcastle, however, responded with great vigour and equalized after 14 minutes when Ephraim Rhodes headed a clearance straight into the path of Howie who slotted the ball home past Naisby.

The rest of the half remained goalless – but never dull – and at the interval it was honours even.

It didn't take Sunderland long to regain the lead after the restart when Veitch could only deflect a shot by Gemmell on to the feet of Bridgett, who again made no mistake, driving home the ball after 48 minutes. Surprisingly it was Sunderland who then laid siege to the Newcastle goal, with Lawrence saving time after time, his performance much appreciated by both sets of supporters, who warmly applauded him. However, there was little he could do to prevent Gemmell scoring a third for Sunderland and effectively sealing the game, although a 66th-minute goal from Orr briefly had the Black Cats rattled.

For Sunderland there were heroes all over the pitch, with Watson outstanding.

As the season progressed people spared a thought for Wolverhampton Wanderers who had an unhappy time in the northeast during the campaign. Thrashed 0-8 by Newcastle at St James' Park on 11th November 1905 – the First Division's highest home win that season – they were also hammered 7-2 by Sunderland at Roker Park on 10th March 1906. It was therefore not surprising to learn that the Midlands team ended at the foot of the table and were relegated, along with Nottingham Forest. Bristol City and Manchester United were promoted, but despite winning two League Championships in 1908 and 1911 the latter, the Red Devils, weren't a particular force to be reckoned with; they became a yo-yo club and wouldn't win the First Division again for some 40 years, by which time Sunderland had six League Championships to their credit.

Tyneside and Wearside's finest met for the return league fixture on 30th December 1905, the last Saturday of the year, at an enlarged St James' Park. The attendance was an enormous

60,000, with 56,000 spectators paying on the day along with 4,000 season ticket holders. The crowd was accommodated with ease, unlike past encounters between the two sides where chaos had often reigned supreme!

Sunderland arrived on Tyneside having won six of the previous seven encounters at the home of their rivals, although the respective league positions – the Magpies lay fifth and the Black Cats 17th in the league table – suggested a home win. Newcastle were strong favourites. However, as is common in local derby games it didn't go to plan, the league positions counted for nothing and Sunderland escaped from Tyneside with a priceless draw.

The Wearsiders' tactics were fairly rudimentary – kick and rush – on the day, as they were overwhelmed by a superior Newcastle side, although, astonishingly, Billy Hogg had given the red and whites the lead after just 10 minutes, with a fine drive that beat the home custodian all ends up. The blame for the Sunderland goal lay fairly and squarely with Carr who had made a hash of clearing Bridgett's centre into the penalty box.

The most unpopular man on the field was undoubtedly Sunderland's David Willis whose rough play drew hoots of derision from the crowd. Rutherford, Newcastle United's tricky winger, was the man made to suffer most as he was fouled time after time.

Inevitably the home side equalized when Sunderland were beaten back into defence and Aitken made an opening that Gardner and McClarence developed so well that Orr was able to equalize after 26 minutes.

Quite how the game remained scoreless for the remaining 64 minutes was a mystery, as wave after wave of Newcastle attacks were somehow thwarted by Sunderland. Indeed, it was generally accepted that once the second half started the visitors had just one thing on their minds – a draw – which they duly got.

Although Newcastle didn't win the FA Cup that season they

came mighty close, finally being beaten 0-1 by Everton in front of 75,609 at the Crystal Palace in the final, having thrashed Grimsby Town and Blackpool en route. Sunderland had gone out in the third round, hammered 0-5 by Woolwich Arsenal, the team that the Magpies had defeated in the semi-final at Stoke City's Victoria Ground. It's worth noting that at that time the likes of Newcastle and Sunderland entered the competition at the first-round stage, rather than the modern-day third round.

The 1906/07 season would be a one to remember for the fans of Newcastle United as the club won their second league title in what was turning out to be a golden decade for the Magpies. By contrast Sunderland under Kyle were finding the going tough, and would end the Football League season in 10th place, a full 14 points behind their Tyneside rivals. Sunderland's problem was clear: they conceded too many goals.

As if to demonstrate this defensive problem the season kicked off at St James' Park with a 4-2 thrashing of Sunderland by the home side; however, for long spells of the game the Wearsiders gave a great account of themselves, taking the lead, and it wasn't until the latter stages of the match that a rampant United made their superior class and firepower tell.

The game was played in an insufferable 90°C heat in front of a crowd of 56,875 who paid ground receipts of £1,575. Newcastle United had a full complement to select from whilst Sunderland gave debuts to Hall, signed from St Mirren, and Tommy Tait, newly acquired from Bristol Rovers. Newcastle took to the field in white shirts.

Sunderland kicked-off, playing against the breeze, and it was Hogg who showed first for the visitors, although it was the debutant Hall who nearly scored, thwarted by Veitch. Though the game was tough it was never dirty but the home side encountered a problem when Aitken and Bridgett clashed, leaving the former with a broken bone in his knee; however, he carried on. The home side's McWilliam was then in the wars as he received a nasty kick from the Black Cats' Gemmell and had to leave the field for a short while for treatment.

Although the game at this point was fairly even the home side took the lead after 27 minutes when Appleyard took a nice pass from Howie and cracked the ball home past a despairing Naisby in the Sunderland goal. He should have doubled the lead a minute later but fluffed the chance. At half-time Newcastle United had a merited lead.

Following the restart Sunderland dominated the play and it came as no surprise when a brilliant run from midfield on 51 minutes led to Bridgett scoring a fine goal, having outpaced his former team-mate McCombie.

The Sunderland forwards then pressed for a second goal, striking the crossbar twice before eventually driving the ball into the net. Lawrence, however, had been charged over and the goal was disallowed. Nevertheless, after 69 minutes Sunderland legitimately took the lead when, handicapped by his damaged knee, Aitken failed to intercept a through ball to Bridgett, who gave his side the lead with another fast ground shot. For several minutes after this Newcastle seemed in a state of collapse and the anxious home crowd wondered whether they could recover.

They did bounce back though in the 77th minute when a sterling effort from Gosnall saw him cross to Rutherford, who scored from a "scrimmage". Five minutes later Appleyard cleverly beat Rhodes and Tait and passed to Rutherford, who scored again. Appleyard missed an open goal in the next minute but with three minutes to go Howie dribbled superbly through the Sunderland defence to score, despite being heavily charged by Watson. Newcastle had completely outplayed Sunderland in the final 15 minutes to gain a fine win.

By the time the two sides met again on 20th March 1907 both of them had been eliminated from the FA Cup; Newcastle after a home defeat to Crystal Palace in the first round and Sunderland to Sheffield Wednesday, also at home, in the last 16. Another game of note had occurred on 19th January 1907 when Sunderland and reigning league champions Liverpool played out a 5-5 draw on Wearside; the game was remarkable due to the fact that the Scouse team had failed to score a solitary goal in their previous five league games.

Newcastle United arrived at Roker Park top of the league but lost 0-2 to a Sunderland side who physically overpowered them on the day. In fact the newspaper reports of the day noted that the home side sailed close to the wind on more than one occasion and were perhaps lucky to end the match with all 11 men on the field.

The attendance was variously reported as anywhere from 32,000 to 35,000 and on a glorious day it was Appleyard who kicked off towards the Fulwell End, with Newcastle defending the Roker End. An even first half ended scoreless although the home side had the upper hand, and there would be no complaints from the Magpies at the end of the game when they were ultimately defeated on merit.

Although Sunderland enjoyed the better second half Newcastle eventually improved and Rutherford had a splendid shot after a pass by Howie. Gardner then miskicked and left the goal wide open to McIntosh and Holley. They raced for goal as Kelsey "pluckily" came to meet them and his kick rebounded off McIntosh and over the bar. The battle was intense and when Rutherford raced clear in the 70th minute he looked to be a certain scorer until he was deliberately tripped by McConnell inside the box and a penalty was quite correctly awarded.

The kick was entrusted to McCracken who fired it low past the post. McCracken loved playing against Sunderland and with 11 appearances in the series holds a record for the Magpies that's unlikely ever to be beaten. Gosnell failed to convert a fine centre from Rutherford and a second chance went begging for United before the Black Cats' Raine outthought McCombie in a run to the goal line, centred, and an exciting scrimmage ensued, during which several sharp shots were sent in until Hogg finally put the ball into the net after 77 minutes. Inspired by this success Sunderland quickly overpowered Newcastle and Raine wasted a glorious opportunity to crown a fine dribble by Bridgett and Holley.

Newcastle played with great spirit, and Gosnell forced two corners in quick succession but they both amounted to nothing. A game-changing moment came with 10 or so minutes left when, in a strong challenge for the ball, Bridgett kicked McCracken severely in the chest and the full-back was carried off. Although Speedie filled the gap, the visitors would end the match with 10 men (remember there were no substitutes in those days). It was hardly surprising that with Sunderland in rampant form they again overwhelmed Newcastle and with a dashing move that saw Holley score a second goal after 85 minutes the red-and-white supporters went home happy.

Prior to league hostilities between the two sides recommencing Newcastle and Sunderland met, in what was fast becoming a rare friendly match, at West Stanley on 9th October 1907. The match, which was brought over from the previous season due to the Geordies' preoccupation with their charge for the league title, was played for the benefit of the Durham Aged Miners' Homes (remember the northeast at that time had coal mining at the heart of its communities). The game attracted a crowd of around 10,000, raising valuable money for the mining association. It was a poor match that the Magpies won fairly comfortably 2-0, with goals in each half from Soye and Hedley.

The 1907/08 season was one where yet again Newcastle United

had a stranglehold on northeast bragging rights. Although the black and whites ended fourth in the table (Manchester United were the league champions) they made it through to the FA Cup final at the Crystal Palace where they met Wolverhampton Wanderers following a 6-0 rout of Fulham at Anfield in the semi-finals. At the final and in front of a crowd of almost 75,000, including the mayor of London, Sir John Bell, who would present the trophy to the winning team, it was the Midlanders who emerged victorious, although not without a scare. Racing into a 2-0 lead United pulled a goal back and it wasn't entirely settled as a contest until five minutes from time when Billy Harrison gave Wolves an unassailable lead. This was all the more welcome as they had ended ninth in the Football League Second Division.

For Sunderland it was another rebuilding season and they would finish 16th in the top flight with just two points separating them from relegated Bolton Wanderers. Again it was the Black Cats' defence that let them down, and in conceding 75 goals they were statistically the leakiest defence in the entire First Division, despite the obvious talents of players such as Bonthron and Daykin.

The first meeting of the two clubs that season took place four days before Christmas Day in 1907. Sunderland were thrashed 2-4 at Roker Park and had gone into the game second from the foot of the league table. In contrast Newcastle were third and were unbeaten in six weeks. For a large proportion of the 30,000 people who attended the match their day had started in chaos as media reports of the day indicated that:

It is estimated the ¾ of the crowd travelled and the service arranged by the NE railway company for the extra traffic to Sunderland completely broke down. There was an extraordinary scene at Newcastle Central station. At 1 pm at least a couple of thousand people were eagerly awaiting transport and there was a fear that they would not arrive in

Sunderland in time for the kick off. An empty train drew up alongside the platform on the South side of the station and immediately there was a wild rush for seats.

Many people were jammed up against the carriages and the pressure was so great that several windows were smashed. The rushing was unseemly and dangerous to all concerned. An even more extraordinary incident occurred on the journey. A train pulled up half a mile outside Monkwearmouth station and the passengers leaped out, swarmed across the rails and over the embankment fences in as direct a line as possible to Roker Park. The public protested vociferously about the inadequacy of the railway service especially as they had paid the ordinary tariff. Some passengers were so long delayed by stoppages that they did not arrive at the ground until long after kick off.

For those that did arrive late it was likely that they missed three or even four goals as Newcastle took an early fourth-minute lead through Rutherford, although this was cancelled out through a Hogg goal three minutes later. Almost from the kick-off Veitch gave the visitors a 2-1 lead. When Rutherford deceived McConnell and Daykin to centre, for Wilson to head home Newcastle's third goal after 24 minutes, the match was effectively over. However, five minutes later Hogg and Holley completely beat McWilliam and Pudan; the ball was crossed to Bridgett who sent a 20-yard volley into the net at express pace to give the home side temporary hope. In the final minute enterprising play by Higgins deceived the defence and he passed to Wilson, who scored with a hard cross shot to seal Newcastle's victory.

The 18th April 1908 was Easter Monday and it was also the week before Newcastle United would take on Wolves in the FA Cup final. As a result the Tyne–Wear derby game saw the home side make changes, although the absence of Pudan from the Magpie starting line-up was an enforced one due to an injury he had picked up on

Good Friday. A crowd estimated at 50,000 turned up to witness Sunderland win once again at St James', as by the time Howie scored for the home side in the 80th minute the Black Cats were home and hosed with goals from George Holley, Arthur Bridgett and Harry Low.

The first half had looked like ending goalless when, five minutes before half-time, Holley burst past McCombie and scored, although just before this goal Sunderland had a scare when their goalkeeper Roose was almost deceived by a bouncing ball from Veitch. The red and whites lost little time in adding to their score after the restart and this time it was Low who was the marksman. McCombie headed out a lofted ball that was met by Low, who fired home a long shot that Lawrence barely saw.

Howie wasted a chance by wanting to walk the ball into the net and Gosnell twice shot wide when well placed. Bridgett scored Sunderland's third goal in his own masterly style when he ran down the wing and took a rising shot. The game slowed down after this and it was evident that Sunderland were prepared to take it more easily. Raybould netted again but was given offside, as was Howie when he converted a pass from the left wing; the referee, however, allowed the goal.

It didn't matter though, Sunderland were the best team on the day and took the two precious points back to Wearside.

The 1908/09 season was another great campaign for Newcastle United. Not only were they crowned league champions for the third time but they also made it to the semi-finals of the English (FA) Cup before being narrowly defeated by Manchester United at Bramall Lane, Sheffield. Sunderland enjoyed a much better season, ended third in the Football League but had the disappointment of losing to Newcastle after a replayed fourth-round English Cup (equivalent of the sixth round in modern times) game.

However, there is one game during the 1908/09 campaign that

will be mentioned until hell freezes over as far as Sunderland fans are concerned and that was the extraordinary meeting between the two sides at St James' Park on 5th December 1908, when the Black Cats emerged victorious 9-1. In telling the tale of one of English football's most remarkable ever top-flight league encounters it is necessary to review the backdrop to the game.

Despite flying high in the Football League table Newcastle United's home game before the one against Sunderland had witnessed a shock 0-2 defeat for the Magpies. Disgusted at what they saw, the directors of the club made wholesale changes to the team line-up for the next away game at Nottingham Forest. Ironically United won 4-0 and with this in mind the St James' hierarchy selected the same team for the game in Nottingham, a decision that, in hindsight, was the Geordies' undoing, although on the face of it there was every justification for doing so. In front of an enormous 60,000 crowd both teams took to the field oblivious to the events that would unfold on that cold December day.

Given the final score, what was perhaps the most remarkable statistic of the day was that the score at half-time was 1-1, although Sunderland took an early seventh-minute lead thanks to Hogg. An even first half wore on as both sides had chances to score but when Newcastle's goal eventually did arrive it wasn't from open play but from the penalty spot after Charlie Thomson, Sunderland's colossus, handled the ball in the penalty area. Shepherd's kick was successful, and a rousing and even half ended all square.

In telling the tale of the second 45 minutes it's probably best to leave it to the media of the time to give the account:

Holley, who was an absolute nonentity in the 1st half sprang into form within 2 minutes of the restart and raced in but was checked. A lamentably weak clearance went straight back to him and a cannon-like drive beat Lawrence easily. Before the cheering had subsided

Holley was off again at full speed to hit the upright. Consternation began to reign in the Newcastle camp at this awakening from such an unexpected quarter. Holley's third attempt at goal inside 5 minutes went wide as Gosnell made a praiseworthy attempt to bolster lost Tyneside confidence.

A brilliant centre saw Duncan battling away at the foot of the upright for an equalizer and only the pluck and brilliance of Roose kept him out. There was still room for optimism as Willis had a powerful drive charged down and it was not until a few minutes later when Sunderland recommenced battering away at the Newcastle door that the plight of the Tynesiders became evident. Their defence was hopelessly beaten, the wing halves were being outpaced and with Whitsun limping badly after being hurt in a melee Pudan was overburdened with work.

Sheer weakness in the United defence brought Sunderland's 3rd goal. Mordue easily avoided a weak tackle and centred from the touchline to give Hogg an easy chance that he took comfortably. Newcastle were facing certain defeat but disaster was to follow. In the 62nd minute Holley got between the full backs to score easily and 5 minutes later he raced in again and scored a glorious goal that made the defence look worse than they really were. After 69 minutes Bridgett ran past the disorganised and distressed Whitsun to drive another goal into the net.

At this stage Whitsun realised he was beyond service to his side and returned to the dressing room. Veitch went to full back and the halfback line lost what little backbone it had. Mordue again beat Pudan to go on himself and score after 73 minutes and 4 minutes later Hogg netted his 3rd and Sunderland's 8th goal. The effect this goal in the 2nd half had on the Sunderland section of the crowd can better be imagined than described. The depressed Newcastle followers could hardly bring themselves to think on the enormity of the defeat inflicted upon their favourites.

Duncan was hurt and carried off a few minutes from the close as Sunderland jubilantly wound up a splendid day's work with another *goal from Bridgett. It was their biggest ever league win against local rivals who sustained a beating the like of which one has never seen and will probably never see again.*

For some reason there appears to be a growing myth developing amongst the Sunderland support that the game was abandoned after 70 minutes, that is, that Newcastle gave up, which clearly wasn't true. On the day and when it was analysed, the one factor that was pointed out over and over was that Sunderland were by far the more physically intimidating side, and simply steamrolled what was essentially half of Newcastle's reserve team.

As a historical footnote Roose, the Sunderland goalkeeper that day, took the match ball home, and its whereabouts remains unknown. I like to think that it is in someone's attic just waiting to be rediscovered. I've often wondered what both Billy Hogg and George Holley thought of not receiving the match ball, although perhaps Roose's decision, a curious one, sorted out a potential tricky situation given that there were two hat-trick men for Sunderland that day.

The 1-9 scoreline remains, over 100 years later, the highest top-flight win in English Football League history. It is also worth noting, that season, Nottingham Forest's 12-0 home defeat of Leicester Fosse at the City Ground in April 1909.

As Sunderland had given such a hiding to their nearest rivals you could be forgiven for thinking that there was a whiff of revenge about the English Cup quarter-final game between the two sides when they were drawn to meet each other at St James' Park just three months later. Again another mammoth crowd, approaching 60,000, watched the match: a thrilling 2-2 draw in which Rutherford gave the home side a 1-0 lead after 14 minutes only to see it cancelled out 60 seconds later by Jackie Mordue. Arthur Brown then scored the best goal of the match to give Sunderland the lead but a mere 60 seconds later United repaid the favour and equalized when George Wilson took advantage of indecision in the visiting defence to slot home past an advancing Roose in the Black Cat goal. In summing up the game the media reported that:

Keen anticipation was more than realised as to the titanic nature of the struggle and it will ever rank as one of the greatest battles between these fierce rivals since they embraced the professional game in the 1880's.

Thanks to the strict control of Referee Mason all suggestion of temper was quickly suppressed and the contest was waged in a thoroughly sportsmanlike manner. Partisan feeling of course manifested itself very strongly and there was always the possibility of some unseemly demonstrations both on and off the field. But the scales of justice were so delicately balanced by Mr Mason that the vast crowd accepted the decisions in the game with unqualified satisfaction.

The fact that neither team was allowed to depart from the principles of the game produced a struggle of Herculean standards and football that has not been surpassed on Tyneside or any other part of the kingdom. How every man mastered the deplorable conditions was a revelation to all critics and confounded the belief the pessimists hold that the nation is decaying in its physical prowess and stamina. There was a fear that Sunderland would take undue advantage of their extra poundage and that the man and not the ball would be the object of their attentions.

They proved however to be law abiding players and used their phenomenal physical power in reasonable support of their splendid footwork. Sunderland gave a superb performance but they encountered men of sterner mettle and experience from those they thrashed 9-1 in December. It was imperative that Newcastle should repair their prestige. From a scientific point of view United have rehabilitated themselves since that debacle though their capacity to play cup football was strongly challenged.

Unparalleled scenes were witnessed outside the ground with queues forming at the gates giving access to the 6d and other unreserved parts of the ground at 10 o'clock. By 12 o'clock the whole of the surrounding area was filled with well behaved, good humoured people who formed up with military precision under the tactful discipline of the police.

There were boisterous spirits but no serious intervention of the police was necessary. The waiting crowd however had a miserable plight. For 2 hours prior to their admission they had to stand submissively in terrible squalls of snow and sleet accompanied by a piercingly cold East wind that must have chilled them to the bone. At last the crowd settled down in their allotted places and an imposing spectacle was presented when the House full signs went up at 2 o'clock.

The replay at Roker Park just four days later was less of a spectacle, and the visitors commanded the game from the start to romp home 3-0 as United entered the semi-finals of the English Cup for the third time in four years.

However, there was some consolation for Sunderland; the official attendance was given as 27,493, with gate receipts amounting to the huge sum of £1,979. This beat the previous best by £732, with the two cup games grossing £4,500 – a lot of money previous to the First World War.

With nothing more to play for as far as Sunderland were concerned, and Newcastle's dreams of an elusive double over following the semi-final defeat to Manchester United, the two teams met for the last time in the Football League that season, just one month later, at Roker Park. Revenge this time was on the minds of the home side and they set about that task in style but only after the dangerous Shepherd had given United a first-minute lead when McWilliam checked Low before hooking the ball over to Shepherd, who deceived Thomson and beat Jarvie, before running in and shooting past Roose. It was a clever goal but as Shepherd was carried off with a damaged leg as a result of the move it seemed as though it had been bought at a high price. He returned after five minutes but never recovered and at half-time he was deemed unfit to carry on.

In the second half Sunderland made some tactical changes: Harry Low went to outside-right with Holley inside and Mordue inside-left with Bridgett on the wing. It had a dramatic effect when, just two minutes after the interval, Brown collected a swinging ball from Holley and steadied himself before firing a tremendous shot into the net from near the penalty spot. Lawrence could not possibly have seen the ball as it flew past him in the 47th minute. Sunderland took the lead only four minutes later when Mordue ran clear and, with the Newcastle defence tottering momentarily, forced a corner. McCracken checked the rush that followed but the watchful Brown was hanging back on the fringe of the struggling crowd. When the ball was forced out he secured it and found an opening for a shot along the ground and into goal. Lawrence was once again unsighted and helpless.

United's Anderson was offside when he volleyed for goal after a "scrimmage" but Roose fielded anything and everything and, above all, Milton shone in timing his challenges to perfection. Wilson, who tried manfully to fill Shepherd's place, went on a brilliant run down the centre and the crowd rose to their feet expecting an equalizer but Milton fairly shouldered him off the ball. In these momentous stages Newcastle fought nobly to retrieve the bad six-minute spell at the start of the second half. Roose saved a great shot from McWilliam but it was Newcastle's last serious effort to save the game.

Thereafter they were beaten in spirit as well as actual play. Brown found McCracken lacking when he sprinted from the halfway line in a swerving run and Whitsun set sail to intercept. Whitsun's tackle left the referee with no option but to point to the penalty spot. Lawrence beat down Holley's kick, but Holley nipped in to net the rebound 17 minutes from the end. Sunderland were beginning to dominate their rivals and Brown found the net once again in the last minute, although it was ruled offside.

So Sunderland recorded their second league victory over Newcastle that season with Roose, Milton, Thomson, Brown and Holley claiming individual honours.

This was Newcastle's first league defeat of 1909 and it carried with it a remarkable coincidence. Since 21st November Newcastle had been beaten on only four occasions. When Sunderland won on 5th December Whitsun was carried off the field for part of the game. When they lost to Manchester United on 26th December McCombie was taken off after only five minutes' play, and when Newcastle played in the semi-final of the English Cup in March Shepherd was a passenger for the whole second half after being hurt.

The last season of the 1900s saw Newcastle United turn the tables on Sunderland by defeating them twice in the league. In September they won 2-0 at Roker Park, an eventful game, and at St James' Park the Magpies triumphed 1-0.

Although United ended the season fourth in the Football League they had a consolation in their first FA Cup win, defeating Barnsley 2-0 at Goodison Park, Liverpool, following a 1-1 draw at the Crystal Palace; the aggregate crowd for the two games was almost 140,000. Coincidentally Sunderland had gone out in the last 16 of the cup, 0-2 to Everton at Goodison.

With Sunderland starting to build an exciting side (they ended the 1909/10 side just a couple of wins from third place), a mammoth crowd rolled up for the first of the Tyne–Wear encounters on 18th September 1909 – a match famous for its off-the-field events rather than being noted for the football on it.

For the record the Magpies, who were superior right from the outset of the match, triumphed 2-0, with goals from Stewart and

Shepherd, but the mere fact that the game went ahead at all was testament to the efforts of the police and the Sunderland secretary (manager) Bob Kyle.

It was evident as soon as the gates opened that the ground would be overwhelmed with spectators and so it proved as (various estimates) between 35,000 and 40,000 turned up to see the football and long before the game had even kicked-off spectators had threatened to spilled over the barriers to get away from the crush.

When the players left the dressing rooms the crowd was so dense that a path had to be cleared to allow them on to the field, although the game started on time and Brown kicked off for Sunderland in bright sunshine.

The first half was about 30 minutes in when the crowd first spilled on to the field at the Fulwell End of the ground (the Roker End being the other "End" at Roker Park). Play was suspended and for almost 15 minutes the players were kept idle while referee Mason, Sunderland secretary Mr Kyle, and the police tried to get the people back behind the barriers. They were assisted by directors and two mounted police.

Before the horses arrived two constables were seen leading a spectator across the ground towards the enclosure. The man proceeded in quite an orderly manner until he approached the centre circle, then a struggle took place and one of the policemen was struck in the face. Finally Mr Kyle joined the trio and persuaded the man to proceed to the enclosure. While this was going on spectators from other parts of the ground rushed on to the field and were even running to and fro across the pitch. The crowd were rather sympathetic to the arrested man and cheered as he went off.

The referee and Sunderland chairman Mr Taylor walked around the ground trying to get the crowd to move back, and eventually play was resumed. This was the signal for one of the horses to start a game of its own and it went prancing across the field, much to the amusement of the spectators. The game was stopped two or three times more, first on account of the horse and later because the crowd again encroached on to the field, especially in the second half when sheer numbers hid the corner flags and lines for an appreciable time.

It was learned afterwards that one of the police horses had been stabbed and the chief constable offered a £5 reward for information leading to the detection of the offender. In view of the stoppages doubts were raised as to whether the match would be allowed to count as a league game but the referee stated at the end that it would count as such. He was also adamant that the full 90 minutes had been played. The United team were advised by the police to make the journey from Tyneside by motor coach, thus avoiding the crush for trams.

As we have already read in earlier chapters the games between the two sides have been characterized by crowd disorder and this was another sad episode, although it also testified once more to the fact that huge crowds were attracted to the fixtures.

Ten days before Newcastle's FA Cup final against Barnsley, Sunderland visited St James' for the final Tyne–Wear derby game of the 1900s. It had been a decade that had belonged to the Magpies, not only from a northeast perspective but also on a wider national scale. The Magpies had been the team to beat.

Newcastle won a fine exhibition of football 1-0 with a goal from Higgins after 86 minutes. The game also doubled up, as was quite customary at the time, as a benefit (testimonial) to the United stalwart Veitch, who gained financially to the tune of £500.

WAR!

1910/11 to 1919/20

If the 1900s had been the decade of Newcastle as far as Tyne and Wear was concerned then the 1910s would be the period where Sunderland re-emerged under Kyle to become a dominant force in English football again. Newcastle would win the top flight just once more in their history, 1926/27, whilst the Black Cats would come close to winning the double in 1912/13 and would claim the league title again in 1935/36. In essence the Geordies would become a cup team with a record to envy, particularly in the 1950s.

The 1st September 1910, the opening day of the 1910/11 season, witnessed Sunderland taking on Newcastle at Roker Park in the first league encounter of the decade. The red and whites triumphed 2-1 – as they deserved to by playing by far the better football – but it was a close run thing.

Sunderland took the lead through George Holley after 32 minutes when Whitson headed a high ball towards his own goal; Mordue collected and worked his way along the goal line before cutting the ball back to Holley who took the ball in his stride and flashed it past Lawrence with the outside of his foot.

Newcastle equalized from the penalty spot with 10 minutes to go, with Shepherd smashing the ball past Roose. The award was not without controversy as the referee consulted the linesman before giving the decision, yet there appeared much more justification for the same punishment a few minutes earlier when Charlie Thomson undoubtedly interfered with the progress of Shepherd.

The decider, with four minutes remaining, came from an accurately placed corner by Bridgett, which Coleman headed into the far corner of the net; indeed Coleman had been unlucky not to score earlier in the game when a screamer from 20 yards had Lawrence at full length and the crowd shouting "Goal" as it flew past the post.

Several special trains from Newcastle, South Shields and all stations in-between were crowded to their capacity as they brought fans from far and wide to the match. As the game was played on a Thursday night with a 5.30pm kick-off thousands of workmen passed through the turnstiles with grimy faces – they had not had time to clean themselves up due to the kick-off time being so soon after they had left the factory and colliery gates.

A mild sensation was created amongst the game's governing authorities by the defiant attitude of players who were wearing an armband bearing the words "Players Union". This signified that they were members of the fledgling Association of Football Players' and Trainers' Union (that later became the PFA), an institution that had been established in 1907 and in 1909 had made it clear to the Football Association that their core objective was to challenge the maximum wage in football.

Given those circumstances, an application by the union to wear the badge was refused by the league executive on the grounds that it might incite feelings and perhaps intimidate players who were not connected with the union. The media of the day reckoned that this would lead to "grave trouble" and in a brief interview a prominent member of the league council remarked (bear in mind the current modern theory on who has the whip hand in football), *"This is a serious breach of discipline and the question will have to be decided as to who are to be the masters, the players or the clubs."* Seventeen Sunderland players had been temporarily suspended by the club when they refused to leave the AFPU in 1909, as were players, famously, from Manchester United. In wearing the armbands they effectively put their careers in jeopardy.

The story of the PFA and the maximum wage was, of course, a story that would rumble on for years to come and was very effectively amplified in the illegal payments scandal that engulfed Sunderland in the 1950s, leading to a fundamental decline at the club from which, some would argue, it took decades to recover.

An interesting innovation was introduced in this game. It was the rubber ball invented by a south country syndicate headed by a Mr Bloomfield. The design was exactly the same as the leather variety but the case was composed of rubber.

It was constructed on the same lines as the outer cover of a bicycle tyre with the base being linen or cotton fabric. Between the inner and outer case there was a lining of felt and, like the rubber-covered ball in golf, it was felt at that time that the propensity of the new football to travel further must inevitably increase the pace of the game. A significant quality was its imperviousness to wet and, unlike the leather-cased ball, its weight was supposed to remain unaltered throughout the worst of the weather. Thus the theory was that players would be saved from serious concussion.

As we now know real developments in ball technology wouldn't come to pass for decades.

The return derby game on 19th November 1910 ended all square with the two goals being scored within three minutes of each other midway during the first half. Once more St James' Park was packed with nearly 60,000 in the ground; however, given the mass unemployment of thousands of workers caused by the lockout of the boilermakers at the shipyards and engineering works it was truly astounding that there was such a huge audience. Half an hour before the start every part of the enclosure was packed with people and the gates were besieged by thousands more. The media reported that *"it was an impressive sight and though partisan feelings ran high the crowd retained its good humour"*. Such was the crowd that the protective barriers snapped like reeds when the crowd in the popular section surged forward to follow the match, but happily no injuries were suffered. A tribute to the sporting conduct of the crowd was paid by Superintendent Carr of the local police force who said *"Nothing happened to call for the intervention of the police."*

It was officially announced that 57,416 people passed through the turnstiles, exclusive of ticket holders, with the receipts being approximately £1,800. This set a new ground record at St James', beating the 53,353 registered for an English Cup tie in 1909. Sunderland went into the game unbeaten so far that season.

The game itself was a beauty and was generally regarded by those old enough to remember way back into the 19th century as one of the best ever between two quality sides. Commenting on the Sunderland side it was stated that their forward line had never looked so balanced since the days of Johnny Campbell; high praise indeed.

Albert Shepherd, who else, scored for the Magpies after 16 minutes, with Coleman equalizing with a rising shot that Lawrence in the Magpie goal could do nothing about.

However, the main talking point of the match was an injury to the Sunderland custodian Roose with 15 minutes to go, following a clash with Rutherford. It resulted in the goalkeeper's forearm being fractured, necessitating treatment at the nearby Royal Victoria Infirmary, a stone's throw from the ground. Arthur Bridgett donned the gloves for the rest of the game and valiantly kept a clean sheet, much to the admiration of the crowd. It was Roose's last ever game for Sunderland. The man who had been part of the 9-1 win just two seasons before saw his footballing career turned on its head at the same venue.

At this point league hostilities between the two ended, with Sunderland ending up third in the First Division, due to a much better defensive record, and Newcastle eighth.

In the English Cup Newcastle once more made it all the way to the final and were narrowly defeated 0-1 by Bradford City at Old Trafford after a replay, following a goalless draw at the Crystal Palace.

The 1911/12 campaign was rather tame by northeast standards. Neither of the clubs produced much football of note and were excluded from the FA Cup, without making much of an impact. League-wise, Newcastle United once more emerged as the better placed of the two sides, ending in third place, five points behind the First Division champions, Blackburn Rovers. The Black Cats finished eighth, five points behind United.

The clubs met three times that season, twice in the league and once in the Newcastle and Sunderland Hospital Cup (also known as the Archibald Cup) on 25th October 1911; the latter raised over £300 for that worthy cause from a disappointing crowd of 11,372. There would be four such matches during the decade, with Sunderland winning three and United just one.

However, it was the first league games between the two, 11 days prior to the charity match, that captured the imagination of both sets of supporters, and at Roker Park 30,000 spectators were thoroughly entertained in an eventful game that saw the visitors triumph 2-1, the winning goal coming from their reserve team player, Scott, just three minutes from time.

Sunderland felt hard done by when a contentious incident inside the penalty area went unpunished: McCracken tackled Gemmell and Holley raced in to blaze the loose ball into obscurity but not before 5,000 Sunderland supporters roared as the ball seemed to hit the United captain's hand. However, the incident escaped the attention of the referee, who was on the blind side and gave the full-back the benefit of the doubt.

For the second time in four years United completed a league double over Sunderland when they triumphed at St James' Park 3-1 in front of 45,000 spectators four months later. The home side never looked back when Tommy Lowes gave them a second-minute lead.

A talking point from the game was the performance of the Low brothers, Harry for Sunderland and Wilf for Newcastle. Harry would serve in the Armed Forces during the First World War, and was honourably discharged, having been wounded. Prior to being called up he had played wartime football for South Shields, retiring from professional football in May 1919 to pursue business interests.

Wilf, who was two years younger, and was nicknamed the Laughing Cavalier, was, like his brother, a Scottish international. He had also started his career with Aberdeen. Football ran in the family as Wilf's son (Harry's nephew) Norman also played professional football, starting out with Liverpool.

Harry Low died in Sunderland on 26th September 1920, aged just 38. His brother Wilf survived him by 13 years, although he too was killed young, knocked down in Newcastle by a car in 1933, aged a mere 49.

Newcastle's second goal came from Anderson after Lowes and Stewart had helped a Rutherford centre across the Sunderland goal. Stewart missed a sitter before collecting a Rutherford centre, outwitting Troughear and scoring the goal of the match for United's third after 81 minutes. Two minutes from the end Harry Low beat Blake from the penalty spot, but it rounded off a poor day for the visitors.

Sunderland didn't deserve anything from the match. Harry Martin was uncharacteristically poor and Milton, normally a stalwart for the Black Cats, had an off day; however, the worst performer by far was Arthur Bridgett, who never got into the game at all.

The 1912/13 campaign saw the re-emergence of Sunderland AFC with a League Championship win and also an FA Cup final appearance. They came as close as anyone could do to winning a first elusive double in the 20th century, a feat that would eventually be achieved by Tottenham Hotspur during 1960/61.

The Black Cats won the league by four points from Aston Villa,

Sunderland's bogey side, the team that would defeat them at the Crystal Palace in front of a world record crowd of 121,919 (also given as 120,081 in some newspapers of the day).

Ironically, the man who scored Villa's winner was Tommy Barber, the right-half, a Geordie who was born in West Stanley towards the outskirts of the Newcastle city limits. Curiously, Sam Hardy, the Aston Villa goalkeeper, had dreamt before the final that Barber would score the winning goal and so it transpired. For Barber, though, near tragedy would strike during his service in the First World War.

At the Somme, Barber was carried from the battlefield, presumed dead, and so a myth perpetuated that he had indeed passed away. In fact, although poisoned by mustard gas Barber made a recovery, turning out for non-league teams such as Stalybridge Celtic and Crystal Palace when hostilities ended. Barber did return to league football briefly with both Merthyr Town and Walsall but his stint didn't last long, the gas taking its toll on his body. He died in 1925, aged just 39.

The title win was all the more remarkable considering Sunderland had lost five and drawn two of their opening seven games. Ironically, the turnaround came in a thrashing of Middlesbrough and from there on in the Black Cats never looked back.

On their way to winning the title Sunderland registered the highest away win that season when they defeated Bradford City 5-0. Villa registered the highest home win that season thrashing the Wednesday (who would become Sheffield Wednesday) 10-0!

Newcastle, in contrast, would have a quieter season than previous, ending 14th in the Football League First Division and being knocked out of the FA Cup quarter-finals by, of all teams, Sunderland, after three gruelling games.

Yet again it didn't take long for the northeast faithful to gather for another Tyne–Wear derby game as, on the opening day of the campaign, 54,215 witnessed a great game between the black and whites and red and whites at St James' Park. One look at the line-ups tells you why matches between the two sides must have involved some wonderful exhibitions of football:

Newcastle United: *Lawrence, McCracken, Hudspeth, Veitch, Low, Hay, Rutherford, McTavish, Shepherd, Hibbert, McDonald.*

Sunderland: *Scott, Troughear, Ness, Cuggy, Thomson, Low, Mordue, Buchan, Richardson, Holley, Martin.*

Frank Cuggy was an interesting character in the Sunderland side. Born a Geordie, in Wallsend, he enjoyed a distinguished career and, once it had finished, he was appointed as the first manager of the newly created Galician side Celta Vigo in Spain in November 1923 on a five-year contract. He met with immediate success, winning the Galician Cup in the 1923/24 season (a national Spanish championship did not commence until 1928).

It was United who went ahead in this encounter after 11 minutes when McDonald rounded Cuggy and, when Troughear advanced, slipped the ball to Hibbert who drew Scott from goal. Shepherd finished the move with a fine shot in off the underside of the bar. At half-time the home side had a deserved 1-0 lead.

Sunderland were aggressive during the greater part of the second half. Their right-wing pair was always in the picture and gave Hay, Hudspeth and Low a harassing time, and it was inevitable that Sunderland would score; that goal duly arrived just seven minutes into the period when a cross from the left saw Mordue reach the ball before Hudspeth. He then outdistanced Wilf Low and Hay before shooting the ball wide of Lawrence and into the net.

Sunderland played like giants in the next 15 minutes – despite

George Holley fluffing an absolute gift when Buchan careered through and centred – and had the United defence not been very steady, a collapse and a beating would have followed.

Nevertheless, at full-time it was generally accepted by a very sporting crowd that a draw was a fair result.

One month later, Sunderland won a Charity Cup game on Tyneside 1-0 in front of only 7,000 before the final league encounter of the season, three days after Christmas at Roker Park.

Without doubt, Sunderland deserved their 2-0 victory at Roker Park. Charlie Buchan was outstanding, as was Wilson for the visitors. Newcastle had a terrific start which unsettled Sunderland, indeed had McTavish not missed a sitter they would have taken the lead.

Once Sunderland got into their stride in the first half they played some excellent football. Buchan's play in particular left the watching England international selection committee representatives present in no doubt that he was the finest inside-right in Britain at that time. It was some display by the Londoner given the ankle-deep mud.

Cuggy saw a fine effort hit the Newcastle upright as did Buchan, and it was the home side who took the lead after 35 minutes when Lawrence saved a shot from Mordue and McCracken looked to have cleared but Holley nipped in and, in the ensuing scramble, whipped the ball into the net.

Just after half-time Newcastle played with 10 men after Little left the field hurt. Buchan had sent in a shot and he took the heavy ball in his stomach from only four yards. He staggered but before he fell cleared his lines. Little was off the field for 15 minutes.

Gladwin rattled the bar with a long drive and it was end to end for a while but with the clock ticking down to 90 minutes it was George Holley who scored his second of the game with four minutes to go. Sunderland broke out of defence when Charlie Thomson intercepted Wilf Low's clearance. The home captain dribbled forward and slipped the ball to Richardson who passed to

Holley and he slotted home.

Although Newcastle were far from disgraced they had now failed to win for the fourth time in eight days.

The main event during 1912/13 between the two sides took place in a nine-day spell between the 8th and 17th of March 1913 when Sunderland and Newcastle met each other three times in a twice-replayed FA Cup quarter-final (equivalent to the modern-day sixth round), which saw the Black Cats eventually prevail but not without a titanic struggle.

The first game was goalless, but never dull, and was watched by a crowd of approaching 30,000. More fans had been expected but Sunderland had doubled the admission fee to one shilling and the gate receipts were £2,026. The Newcastle fans travelled in their thousands from Tyneside and the majority were at the turnstiles by midday.

It was a reasonable game, one that Shepherd missed, and one or two fans of a red-and-white persuasion were heard to chant in dirge-like tones "1, 2, 3, 4, 5, 6, 7, 8, 9" in an obvious reference to the 1-9 game at St James' Park, in an attempt to wind up the opposition. However, at the end of the struggle it was left to Newcastle's McCracken to sum up, saying that *"It was an excellent game with not a great deal in it but that was in our favour. I think we ought to have won."*

As expected there was huge interest in the replay at St James' Park. Over 56,000 turned up and the gates were closed half an hour before the advertised start to ensure that there would be no repeat of the overcrowding that had marred previous Tyne–Wear encounters on Tyneside. Ultimately, it was estimated that some 15,000 fans were locked out.

Newcastle had to reorganize their forward line due to injuries to Rutherford and Stewart. McDonald and Wilson retained their places but Shepherd was brought in at centre-forward and McTavish and

Hibbert formed the right wing. Shepherd, occasionally bothered by the nasty knee laceration received in a terrible collision with Ashcroft two years ago, was weakened in a tussle with the robust Milton in the first half and five minutes after the interval he was practically a passenger; he was consigned to the right wing where he waited Micawber-like for stray balls. With Mordue pronounced fit Sunderland were represented by what was generally accepted as their best 11.

It was the home side who took the lead after 16 minutes. McTavish's swift and stylish advances down the touchline brought a throw-in. Hibbert sent the ball across and McTavish carried it through into the net. Tumultuous crowd scenes ensued as the Newcastle supporters' joy knew no bounds, but after 28 minutes Sunderland drew level and their supporters' delight made for an extraordinary spectacle when George Holley bored his way through the Newcastle defence and shot a goal past Lawrence. There was a suspicion that the ball had been elbowed to him by Richardson but the referee ruled that the ball had flown off the centre-forward's shoulder. The 1-1 score at the interval was a fair reflection of the play.

In the second half the United forward line was weakened by an ankle injury to McDonald. But despite limping he courageously persevered and played well given his handicap. The game developed into a titanic struggle but Sunderland looked to have snatched it at the death when Charlie Buchan – who else – scored from a corner kick with just three minutes remaining. However, even before the travelling red-and-white hordes' jubilation had subsided, the home side were level when Wilf Low placed a free-kick to Veitch who collected the ball and whacked it hard and true through a ruck of players. To the dismay of his Sunderland team-mates the normally unflappable giant Charlie Gladwin, in attempting to clear, diverted the ball out of Butler's reach and into his own goal. An extra half hour failed to decide the issue and it was mutually agreed to replay at St James' Park after tossing a coin for choice of venue.

Burnley, awaiting the winners in the semi-final, would have to wait a bit longer to find out who their opponents would be.

After this game a curious story emerged. Charlie Gladwin, the huge Sunderland right-back, had left St James' Park and taken a tram (the system ran through the city from 1887 to 1950) that travelled through Newcastle centre. A Newcastle United fan, talking loudly on the tram, made it known to all who would listen that Gladwin had deliberately scored the own goal, insinuating that he had taken a bribe. Overhearing this remark Gladwin bided his time and, when the tram came to a standstill at the next stop, an altercation took place, which resulted in Charlie punching his accuser and knocking him off the tram.

Five days later Sunderland settled the affair with a fairly comfortable 3-0 win at St James'. However, Newcastle were handicapped for the game. An ankle injury forced Rutherford out of the match and McDonald and Shepherd were also incapacitated. This forced United to reconstruct their entire forward line, with Duncan at outside-right and Hibbert being flanked by Stewart and Wilson.

The attendance was 49,354 and the receipts amounted to £2,075. No fewer than 134,245 people had paid to see the three games and the receipts came to £6,650 – a huge figure in those days.

The strong wind that Newcastle had to face was a handicap but it was nothing compared to the snowstorm which raged for most of the first half. With the wind and snow at their back Sunderland scored twice.

The first goal after eight minutes was directly due to the wind and a bouncing ball. There was a misunderstanding in the United defence as both Low and McCracken went for the ball as it bounced through to Holley. The Black Cats' ace marksman came off best and beat Lawrence with a cross shot that curled into the net.

The 40th-minute penalty was deserved as Veitch clearly tripped Harry Low when he was almost up to the goal. Mordue's rising shot from the spot was a goal as soon as it left his foot. It was the first penalty scored against United that season, with Lawrence having saved all the others that had been conceded.

Jimmy Lawrence was an excellent goalkeeper for Newcastle and his record of 498 appearances (plus nine wartime appearances and 174 clean sheets) over an 18-year period has yet to be surpassed by any Magpie.

The third goal after 75 minutes came from a breakaway by Martin. The Newcastle half-backs and also McCracken had been lying well up the field to break up the attacks of the Roker forwards when the ball came out to Martin. He raced away at top speed and his centre went straight to the man from Edmondsley, Jackie Mordue, who collected and moved in on goal. Lawrence advanced but was beaten by Mordue's flighted shot and that was the issue settled.

In the aftermath of the game the Football Association fined Newcastle United £150 for fielding an under-strength side.

Including the Charity Cup game the two teams had played each other six times during the 1912/13 campaign, with Newcastle winning none of the encounters.

The tables would be turned just one season later when Newcastle did the league double over Sunderland, whilst the Black Cats had the consolation of another charity match win.

The game at Roker Park in September 1913 drew a crowd of 45,000 and resulted in a 2-1 win for the visitors. Ground improvements had been carried out to increase capacity at Roker, however, not all areas of the new concrete stand were ready in time. The defeat was partially self-inflicted after Harry Low had missed a 60th-minute penalty; Lawrence in the Newcastle goal saved it, as he did in the Tyne–Wear derby game of 1908/09.

In early action George Holley was hit full in the face by a shot from his own team-mate Harry Martin after five minutes and was knocked out, but he recovered well to put Sunderland ahead after eight minutes. In doing so Holley scored his 15th league and cup goal against Newcastle, which stands to this day as a record for any individual player in the Tyne–Wear derby series. The equalizer came in the 44th minute after fine play by Hall. He received the ball 10 yards into the Sunderland half and beat off challenges by Cuggy and Gladwin before driving a fine left-foot shot along the ground and just inside the upright. There were some extraordinary incidents in the second half, as within five minutes of the restart Findlay fouled Buchan two yards inside the penalty area, and Mr Taylor gave a free-kick just outside the box.

Then, after 60 minutes, Richardson raced goalwards with Low on one side of him and Hudspeth on the other. As soon as Low stuck out his foot to touch the ball away Richardson fell full length, and the referee who had erred earlier in refusing Sunderland's just demand for a penalty now penalized a perfectly fair tackle. Low took the kick and lobbed rather than shot the ball straight at Lawrence, who cleared. Gradually Newcastle began to take command, and nine minutes from the end King and McDonald launched a clever attack. McDonald sent over a perfect centre and King fired in the winner.

After giving a feeble display against Bradford City on Boxing Day, Newcastle played well against Sunderland at St James' Park two days after Christmas and thoroughly deserved their 2-1 victory to end Tyne–Wear hostilities for the 1913/14 campaign. Newcastle went into the match without one of their forwards having scored a league goal since 15th November, when Hall scored against Tottenham. A newspaper report summed up the events, writing that *"the formbook favoured Sunderland but their defeat was as complete as it was possible to be".*

In a goalless first half disappointment reigned when Hudspeth sent in a brilliantly taken free-kick that flashed downward from the bar, and then Goodwill failed to hit the target with the goal at his mercy from just six yards out. It had been a tale of the oft-repeated Newcastle forward supremacy and no goals. Then came the change, and nine minutes after the restart George Holley handled the ball. From a neatly taken free-kick Goodwill sent a fine first-time shot into the net for his first league goal. After 75 minutes Bert Hobson handled while stopping Wilson's progress four yards outside the penalty area, and Hay sent over the free-kick. Douglas knocked the ball back across goal and Hibbert's head got there just in time to deflect it past Butler. There was a consolation for Sunderland in the last minute when Hudspeth headed Martin's cross out for a corner and from this Buchan got Sunderland's goal.

The Black Cats ended the First Division season as northeast top dogs, finishing seventh in the table, four points ahead of the Magpies, who were in 12th position. In the FA Cup Sunderland thrashed Chatham in the first round proper, 9-0, whilst Newcastle were on the wrong end of a 0-5 home drubbing against Sheffield United at the same stage. Sunderland would eventually succumb to the eventual winners, Burnley, in the quarter-finals.

The 1914/15 Football League season started with Great Britain at war with Germany, following a complicated set of circumstances that had at the heart of it the crumbling of what could be best described as imperialist empires. A trigger point came on 28th June 1914, when a Bosnian-Serb student and member of the Young Bosnia political group assassinated the heir to the Austro-Hungarian throne, Archduke Franz Ferdinand of Austria, in Sarajevo, Bosnia.

Therefore the 1914/15 season, in which again the Tyne–Wear rivals met three times, twice in the league and once in the Charity Cup (Sunderland winning the Newcastle and Sunderland Hospital Cup for the third successive year), was the last competitive football between the two sides until 1919/20.

The first league encounter came at St James' Park on 25th December 1914. Sunderland routed Newcastle 5-2 and, coupled with their previous victory – a 6-0 trouncing of Tottenham Hotspur at White Hart Lane six days earlier – it was fair to describe the Black Cats' strikers as being in "good form".

The home side's two goals were own goals, both coming within two minutes of each other, and the scoring could have been improved had Newcastle's Hudspeth not missed a 20th-minute penalty.

On a frost-bound pitch Bobby Best scored a hat-trick for Sunderland, the highlight of his Sunderland career. One newspaper reported that *"in attack it was the brilliance of Best that was the outstanding feature of the game"*. However, as we shall see shortly, Best would go from hero to zero, as in the return match at Roker Park the following day he missed a penalty.

Best scored for Sunderland after eight minutes, and with the game 20 minutes old Douglas was brought down by Cringan in the penalty area when racing for goal. Mr Howcroft, the referee, gave a penalty to Newcastle but Hudspeth drove wide. Then, after 31 minutes, Best took Mordue's pass and beat three defenders to score, while, within a minute of half-time, Buchan intercepted a clearance from a Newcastle defender and drove hard and true into the net.

Now 3-0 down at half-time, and having missed a penalty, things were pretty bad for the home side – but were about to get worse. Finding McCracken in two minds Best appeared on the scene and punished the full-back's hesitancy with a fourth goal four minutes into the second half. Then Phillip scored a fifth goal after 70 minutes with a shot that Lawrence touched but failed to stop. This ended the tide of disaster as far as Newcastle were concerned and after 73 minutes a corner kick by Goodall was turned into his own net by Scott to reduce the deficit. Two minutes later Ness passed to

Scott who had come out to help the full-back and the ball lobbed into the net.

Walter Scott in the Sunderland goal was a controversial character who was prone to error and was eventually sacked by the directors of the club for "palpable inefficiency".

In the return game at Roker Park the next day Newcastle again triumphed, this time 4-2. However, Sunderland were their own worst enemy, with not only Best but Jackie Mordue missing a penalty.

First blood went to United after five minutes when Hewison forced a corner. Wilson placed the ball beautifully and although the home defence cleared it was fired back in by Hudspeth from long range and dropped nicely into the net, with Scott unable to reach it. This was the signal for determined attacks by Sunderland and after 10 minutes of play it paid dividends when Thomson crossed to Mordue who, running in, sent a swift low shot out of Mellor's reach. Sunderland's success merely spurred Newcastle on and Douglas then crossed to Higgins, who drove the ball into the net six minutes later. Sunderland attacked vigorously and were seemingly rewarded for their endeavour after 19 minutes when Phillip sent the ball sailing towards the Newcastle goal. Mellor was well off his line and McCracken did the only thing he could in the circumstances and handled the ball. This turned out to be a smart move as Mellor smartly saved Mordue's penalty kick.

Charlie Buchan then levelled the scores from Mordue's well-placed corner kick after 20 minutes, and at half-time the scores remained level.

The Newcastle goal, however, had a charmed existence in the early stages of the second half, particularly as Hay infringed when checking Mordue close to it and another penalty kick followed. Best missed the goal altogether, technically the only time that Sunderland has ever missed a penalty against Newcastle as the others that did not score were all saved. Buchan then headed against the upright and Mordue missed an easy chance before Douglas put Pailor free right in front of the Sunderland goal, however, the chance was wasted.

There was no more scoring until the 75th minute when Hibbert gave Newcastle the lead again by scoring two goals in quick succession. He was well placed and totally unmarked when he converted a pass from Douglas for the first, and three minutes later he headed another into the net.

The day couldn't have been much worse for Sunderland as even before the game kicked off the club had experienced misfortune. They discovered that a fire had broken out in Bob Kyle's office and the fire brigade had to be called.

There was widespread dismay in Great Britain about the playing of competitive football whilst soldiers were dying for their country on the battlefield and therefore the Football League and the FA Cup were suspended from the end of 1914/15 until 1918/19, although Newcastle and Sunderland did play eight friendly War Fund and Victory League matches during that period, with Sunderland winning five of them.

The story of the intervening war years was therefore one of catastrophe for Europe and, in respect of this book, football. Both Newcastle and Sunderland provided loyal servants to their country in a brutal war, with some never returning to their families, never mind the sport.

The official history of Newcastle United states that six of their players died in the First World War, including Thomas Goodwill, Dan Dungilson and Tom Hughes. Goodwill and Dungilson both joined the 16th Battalion Northumberland Fusiliers (Newcastle Commercials); both were killed on 1st July 1916 in the attack on Thiepval. They are commemorated on the Thiepval Memorial in France, which is a permanent tribute to the 72,191 British and South Africans whose bodies were never recovered from the Battle of the Somme.

Tom Hughes is harder to trace but there was a casualty of that name in the 27th Northumberland Fusiliers (Tyneside Irish) who was killed in action (KIA), again on 1st July 1916. This means that two Newcastle United players were killed on the first day on the Somme, and possibly three; all in fairly close geographic proximity.

Three other former Magpies were killed during the war, one of which also had an association with Sunderland AFC.

Captain Tom Rowlandson MC, Yorkshire Regiment, was KIA on 15th September 1916 and is buried in Bécourt Military Cemetery in the Somme. He was an amateur who played in goal for Sunderland, Newcastle, Corinthians and England, and he received the Military Cross. The club history names a fifth player, Major John Fleming, East Yorks Regiment, as KIA in 1917. He played for the club between 1911 and 1913 and afterwards for Spurs. The last club fatality, but undoubtedly the most famous military-wise, was Donald Bell VC.

Few acts of gallantry could match that of Donald Simpson Bell, the first professional English footballer to enlist in the First World War, who was posthumously awarded the Victoria Cross.

Second Lieutenant Bell earned Britain's highest military decoration for valour for wiping out a German gun post, only to die five days later in the Battle of the Somme on 10th July 1916.

His association as a United player came in the reserves when he most notably assisted Newcastle to win the Hospital Cup in 1911 against Spen Black and White.

The *London Gazette*, 9th September 1916, told of his award:

La Boiselle, Somme, France, 5 July 1916, T / Second Lieutenant Donald Simpson Bell, 9th Bn, The Yorkshire Regiment.

For most conspicuous bravery (Horseshoe Trench, France). During an attack a very heavy enfilade fire was opened on the attacking company by a hostile machine-gun. Lieutenant Bell immediately, and on his own initiative, crept up a communication trench and then, followed by Corporal Colwill and Private Batey, rushed across the open under heavy fire and attacked the machine gun, shooting the firer with his revolver, and destroying gun and personnel with bombs.

This very brave act saved many lives and ensured the success of the attack. Five days later this gallant officer lost his life performing a similar act of bravery.

Donald Bell's Victoria Cross and campaign medals had been on a long loan to the Green Howards Museum in Richmond, Yorkshire, but were sold at auction by Spink of London on 25th November 2010. The group realized a sale hammer price of £210,000. They were purchased by the Professional Footballer's Association and are on display at the National Football Museum in Manchester.

Along the road in Sunderland, the football club said goodbye, permanently in two cases, to a few of their current and former players.

Harry Low who, as was recorded earlier in this book, was the brother of Newcastle United's Wilf, served in the Armed Forces during the First World War and was honourably discharged, having been wounded.

Harry Martin served in the Army and, on the cessation of hostilities returned to Sunderland, where he continued to play into the 1920s before being transferred to Nottingham Forest – he had guested briefly for the latter during the First World War.

Bert Hobson saw active service, winning the Military Medal for bravery.

Albert Milton was born in Sheffield in 1885 and played football for South Kirkby. In 1907 he was transferred to Barnsley, for whom he played just 15 games before attracting the attention of Sunderland, who bought him in 1908 for £350.

He made his red-and-white debut at Ayresome Park in a 3-0 away victory in which Jackie Mordue scored twice and Alf Common, once famously of Sunderland, missed a penalty. Ironically it was Milton who handled in the box, trying to stop Wilcox from scoring.

Charlie Buchan described Milton as "five foot six and a half inches of solid manhood, with thighs like tree trunks and the courage of a Lion. He was a grand player and a staunch colleague."

Milton played 27 league games during the 1912/13 season but, heartbreakingly for him, having played in the first seven FA Cup ties, he missed out on the last two through injury. His place was taken by Harry Ness.

On the outbreak of the First World War hostilities Milton worked in a munitions factory, turning out for Sunderland Rovers, when available, in 1915. He was called up to the Royal Field Artillery (attached to the Durham Light Infantry) and made his way to Flanders to fight in the slaughter of Passchendaele. The day before the main attack, 11th October 1917, Bombardier Milton was killed in action, aged just 31.

He is remembered at the Tyne Cot Memorial, one of four to the missing in Belgian Flanders, which covers the area known as the Ypres Salient, maintained in perpetuity by the Commonwealth Graves Commission.

In an ironic twist, Milton probably fought within a few miles of his former team-mate at Sunderland, Charlie Buchan, who survived all three of the Ypres bloodbaths.

Perhaps, though, the Black Cats' most famous two players on the Western Front were the aforementioned Charlie Buchan and Leigh Richmond Roose.

Buchan served with the Grenadier Guards. On being given lance corporal status he ended up fighting on the Western Front at the Somme, Cambrai and Passchendaele, three of the bloodiest conflicts of the First World War. That he survived all three to tell the tale is a feat in itself, that he was also decorated for his bravery made his *Boy's Own* story complete.

In his autobiography, *A Lifetime in Football*, he modestly makes little mention of his war record, and the events surrounding his decoration are never given. However, research reveals that when Buchan's unit was pinned down in battle he stormed a German lookout post with his troops close behind him. They took the lookout post but, in doing so, Buchan was bayoneted in the foot by the one German soldier who had remained alive. Luckily for Buchan the bayonet went straight through the gap between his toes. The fate of the German soldier is unknown.

His commendation was ensured when, under enemy fire, he went back to the mess tent to get his men food as their rations had run out. His successful achievement of this was presumably helped by the fact that he was a fast runner.

Buchan's Military Medal was gazetted on 12th December 1917, won presumably at Cambrai, some seven miles behind the Hindenburg line, which had been fought the month before. There was no citation with his medal but he was nominated for a commission shortly afterwards.

The Battle at Cambrai is significant in that it was the first time that tanks, some 400 of them, had been used in such number in a war. To place Buchan's good fortune and bravery into perspective, the Germans suffered 50,000 casualties and the British 45,000.

The story of Roose is part uplifting and part tragic.

A remarkable man, Roose was born on 26th November 1877 in Holt, five miles east of Wrexham, Wales. His father, Richmond Leigh Roose, was a Presbyterian minister in the village. It is almost certain that his father would have kept company with the iconic writer H G Wells who worked as a teacher at Holt Academy at the same time. More than a mere goalkeeper, Roose was also a renowned socialite, playboy, trainee physician and soldier of his day. As a true maverick his brushes with authority became legendary. He is widely regarded as one of the finest footballers that Wales has ever produced.

At the age of 16 Roose was accepted to study at the University of Wales, Aberystwyth, where he wanted to study medicine. However, it wasn't long before he became better known as a remarkably talented goalkeeper for the university football team. By 1899 he was good enough to be mentioned as a possible selection for the Welsh national team, eventually making his debut for them against Ireland in the Home International Championships. Roose followed this up with an appearance for Aberystwyth Town in the Welsh Cup final of 1900 against Druids from Ruabon, where he picked up a winner's medal in a 3-0 romp.

Roose moved to London, and by 1901 his performances in goal for club and country were attracting the attention of professional clubs; so much so that he signed for Stoke City in October of that year. In a fixture at Manchester City Roose saved a penalty, gestured to the crowd and had an apple thrown at him. So began a maverick career that contained many legendary stories. Included was a visit to Sunderland where one of the home directors made fun of the Stoke team. Roose's reaction was to punch the man in the mouth; he was severely censured by the FA once the incident became public. It was therefore ironic when he signed for Sunderland in January 1908.

The events surrounding Roose's eventual death would remain a mystery for almost 90 years. The good doctor had been assigned to the 9th Royal Fusiliers in France during the First World War, following a spell as a military medic in Turkey. On 28th August 1916 he was awarded the Military Medal for bravery, having been part of a successful Allied attack on the Germans at a place known as Ration Trench, and was promoted to the rank of lance corporal. Well known to all of his comrades at arms he became embroiled in the Battle of the Somme and, following 99 days of consecutive fighting, died on the Western Front on 7th October 1916, mown down by a machine gun. His comrades saw him fall into a bomb crater, although as far as his family were concerned they had been told that Roose was missing in action, presumed dead, following his participation at Gallipoli in 1915. However, the misspelling of Roose's name as "Rouse" in the official British War Records did not reveal his true fate until December 2006. The legendary Leigh Richmond Roose is remembered at Thiepval, the largest British war memorial in the world, which was designed by the influential architect Sir Edwin Lutyens.

The Armistice that ended the First World War was signed in a railway carriage on 11th November 1918, although full peace was not ratified until 10th January 1920. The Football League recommenced in 1919/20, and it didn't take long for Newcastle and Sunderland to renew their rivalry in what were the last two games between the sides in that decade.

Hostilities resumed on 22nd November 1919, with a 2-0 win for Sunderland at Roker Park in front of nearly 50,000 people, the biggest ever Tyne–Wear derby attendance on Wearside soil at that time. It was estimated that another 10,000 people were locked out.

The Black Cats were the better side and, indeed, their keeper Allan didn't have one decent shot to save, such was the powder-puff nature of the United attack. Both the Sunderland goals were scored by Charlie Buchan, after 17 and 47 minutes. For the first goal Harry Martin should not have been allowed to get clear. He was left with an open field and he closed right in before crossing to Buchan, who headed past the helpless Bradley. Best started the move for the second goal and left Buchan with a fine opening. Buchan sped goalwards and, as the angle narrowed, seemed in two minds whether to centre or shoot. Bradley read his mind and appeared to be leaving himself the chance to recover in case of a centre. However, Buchan shot with tremendous power and although Bradley made a great effort he failed to stop the ball's progress into the net.

At the return league game, played one week later at St James' Park, Sunderland again emerged triumphant, continuing their good record on Tyneside. This time the Black Cats won 3-2 in front of an enormous crowd of nearly 62,000. Newcastle dominated the early proceedings but had to wait until the 38th minute to go ahead through Hibbert. Wilf Low sent in a long shot and Allan, the Sunderland custodian, gathered the ball but seemed at a loss what to do with it. He twisted and turned and ended up facing his own net, and Hibbert eventually kicked the ball out of his hands and into the net. The second goal came five minutes later when Hall's shot had been half stopped by Allan, and as he came out to try and complete the clearance Robinson flashed the ball past him.

At half-time it looked a long way back for Sunderland but Newcastle made the classic mistake of sitting back on their lead – and paid dearly for it. The visitors reduced the arrears after 62 minutes when a long centre by Martin was headed away by Hibbert, but the ball was too high for him to get it away properly. He merely turned the ball into the path of Jackie Mordue, who scored with a first-time shot. Sunderland drew level with 15 minutes to play when Frank Cuggy's pass enabled Travers to deliver a shot on the run, which nestled firmly in the back of the net. The miraculous comeback was complete with five minutes remaining when Travers dashed ahead of Hudspeth, who was slow in getting to him, and scored his second goal of the game.

Sunderland ended a turbulent decade in fifth place, well behind the eventual First Division champions West Bromwich Albion, with Newcastle finishing eighth. In the FA Cup neither side made much of an impression. Sunderland made the last 16 but were eliminated by their bogey team, Aston Villa. Newcastle went out narrowly at home 0-1 to Huddersfield Town.

THE ROARING TWENTIES

1920/21 to 1929/30

The Roaring Twenties was a remarkable period in the Tyne–Wear rivalry as it was the last where the two teams played each other for league points in every season of that decade. This would, of course, be due to two factors: two world wars and also relegation for one or the other of the two teams, usually Sunderland, who were relegated an incredible nine times between 1957 and 2006, five of those times since 1986.

The 1930s would bring only eight competitive fixtures and the 1940s just four, although there would be various games played between the sides during the Second World War, including an improvised version of the FA Cup. Incredibly, in the 1980s there would be just four league encounters between the teams, supplemented by two absorbing play-off games.

For Sunderland the 1920s was a frustrating decade which produced no trophies but plenty of near misses. To place that into perspective they finished in the top four on no fewer than five occasions, due to outstanding players such as Charlie Buchan, who would leave part-way through the decade, and then ace marksman David Halliday, one of the most potent goalscorers ever in English football.

Although Newcastle couldn't match Sunderland's top-four tally they could boast about a League Championship in 1927, the last time the club would win the English top flight. They could also brag of one of their all-time great players, Hughie Gallacher, as the famous quote/song went, *"the wee Scots lad, the best centre forward Newcastle ever had"*, who played for the Geordies between 1925 and 1930, scoring almost a goal a game for them.

Gallacher would ultimately be offered to Sunderland by the Newcastle directors in May 1930 when it was revealed that *"the other ten players did not see eye to eye with him"* and as the Roker directors declined him, he would eventually be sold to Chelsea later that year.

For once there were no friendlies played between the two sides, just 20 competitive and absorbing league encounters that thrilled some massive crowds.

The first of those games took place on 9th October 1920 and ended as a 6-1 routing of Sunderland at St James' Park played in front of 61,000 people. To place the attendances for Tyne and Wear derby games into perspective at this time, over 1 million people watched the 20 league games between the two sides in the decade.

The damage to Sunderland was done in a 14-minute spell either side of half-time when Newcastle scored five times, including one goal from the legendary Stan Seymour who played almost 250 times for the Geordies during the decade and would serve them in other capacities in a long association with the football club, earning him the nickname of "Mr Newcastle United". To compound Sunderland's misery Bert Hobson missed a penalty. However, Charlie Buchan scored a consolation goal for Sunderland after 50 minutes.

Sunderland should have taken the lead after 20 minutes when a penalty was given against Billy McCracken for bringing down Harry Martin as he broke through. However, Hobson shot straight at Lawrence who punched the ball away. Newcastle's first goal was a cracker by Smailles after 33 minutes, who played an unstoppable shot past Leslie Scott, after a perfect centre from Stan Seymour.

The ball struck the underside of the bar before entering the net and the on run of play Newcastle deserved the lead. Ten minutes later the home side doubled their lead when Seymour shot at the unattended goal and Joe Kasher used his hands to prevent a goal. Neil Harris was entrusted with the penalty and beat Scott to give United a 2-0 interval lead.

Newcastle's third goal came just three minutes into the second half from Harris, when he capitalized on a great pass from Seymour to give Scott no chance. Two minutes later the advantage was reduced with a typical Charlie Buchan goal, a header, following good work from Harry Martin. Smailles scored a fifth goal with a header off Seymour's pass, and with two minutes remaining brilliant work by Billy Aitken brought about a sixth goal scored by Ted Ward.

Incredibly this was the first time that Newcastle United had ever defeated Sunderland by more than two clear goals in a competitive match.

Only one week later, in front of an estimated crowd of 45,000, Newcastle claimed a league double over Sunderland at Roker Park, winning the encounter 2-0. The attendance was lower than expected, this being put down to the fact that it was during a coal miners' strike, one of several that took place during the 1920s. Another factor was that many fans anticipated a crush inside the ground and therefore didn't bother to attend due to safety concerns.

In an eventful half it was surprising that it ended all square, but two goals in 11 minutes gave the game to the visitors.

The first goal came when Stan Seymour stooped to head a centre from Aitken into the corner of the net and the second, just before the hour mark, started with Bob McIntosh who took the ball from Cooke and sent Aitken away. He beat Ernie England and centred perfectly for Neil Harris to strike the ball past Scott, the home custodian.

The league encounters the following season again came within a week of each other, this time in November. Honours were even in both games, including a rare goalless draw.

The first game on Tyneside drew a crowd of around 45,000, which was well down on pre-match estimates but a good attendance given the poor weather. Newcastle had an experimental side out and few Newcastle fans expected much from their favourites. However, they rose magnificently to the occasion and matched Sunderland in every department in what was an excellent game. Buchan was in his prime for Sunderland and much was expected from him.

The game had a sensational start when the home side went two up after just seven minutes: McIntosh and then McDonald doing the damage. However, Buchan, despite being controlled by Wilf Low for most of the game, did get away twice in the match and both times his class told as he headed the first goal after a cross from Harry Martin after 51 minutes and then presented Bob Marshall with an opportunity too good to miss five minutes later.

The second game at Roker Park was played out in front of just under 50,000 supporters and ended scoreless; for the first time in history the Tyne–Wear rivals shared the points in both games in one season. A newspaper report following the match stated:

There was no score and this was a true reflection of the play. There were times when Sunderland dominated play but Newcastle played the scientific football and Sunderland the robust but neither appeared to gain any great advantage from the tactics. It was a case of defences on both sides being too strong for the attacks.

Men of the match were Wilf Low for Newcastle, who again shackled Buchan well, and Ernie England for Sunderland.

The season 1921/22 was a poor one, league-wise, for the two teams, with Newcastle ending the season seventh and Sunderland a few points behind in 12th. Newcastle did, however, have the consolation of the biggest away win that season, defeating Birmingham 4-0 in January 1922.

Similarly, in the FA Cup it was pretty much a tale of woe as Sunderland crashed out in the first round proper, 0-5, after a replay against Liverpool. Newcastle fared little better and were eliminated in the second round proper at Preston North End.

The 1920s produced some excellent contests between the two sides, none more so than that one season later when, at St James' Park, the Geordies won 2-1 in a match played out in front of around 60,000 spectators. Once more Buchan was well marshalled, this time by Mooney.

At least 6,500 Sunderland fans made the short trip, including 1,500 who walked the 12 miles to witness their favourites, who before the match lay in second place in the Football League behind Liverpool. Prophetically this is how the league would end, with the Black Cats six points adrift of their Merseyside rivals.

Newcastle just about deserved their win although it might have been bigger had Harris not had a goal disallowed for offside. The Magpies, however, took the lead after 35 minutes when Aitken headed through from Seymour's corner kick.

Newcastle kept on pressing and Warney Cresswell had to clear a Harris shot off the line with Ted Robson, the Sunderland custodian, well beaten. Sunderland levelled close to the hour mark when Buchan drove the ball past Bradley. With 15 minutes to go Newcastle scored what proved to be the winner when McDonald caught the Sunderland defence napping and flicked the ball past Robson.

For some in the crowd the final whistle came as a relief. It was later reported that dozens of spectators had received crush injuries, although fortunately few were seriously hurt.

The game at St James' was clouded in controversy. On arriving at Roker Park on the Monday before the game Charlie Buchan was presented with a letter, on which was written *"You will be paid £1,000 if you lose the game at Newcastle."* The maestro gave the letter to the chief constable of Sunderland who opened up an investigation and traced the author: an inmate of an asylum in Bristol!

Sunderland gained revenge a week later at Roker Park when goals from "Tricky" Hawes and Paterson within 10 minutes of each other gave the red and whites a much needed win and kept Sunderland in touch at the top of the table.

The game hinged on an incident after 34 minutes when Mooney was accidentally struck in the stomach by Sunderland's Hunter; he couldn't continue and the visitors played for nearly an hour with just 10 men. A resulting reshuffle meant that Buchan had pretty much unfettered access to do as he pleased. He didn't need a second invitation as he probed and prompted all afternoon.

Sunderland were dominant for most of the game, so much so that a newspaper reported:

Bradley kept a magnificent goal saving all manner of shots but he was spared a lot of anxiety by the sure kicking and tackling of Hampson and Hudspeth. Had any of this trio faltered then another 9-1 debacle might easily have been the result.

"Tricky" Hawes got the home side's first goal two minutes after the interval, heading a centre by Donaldson past Bradley, although the visiting custodian was hampered when going for the ball. He had no chance 10 minutes later with Paterson's drive from 10 yards after Buchan had neatly set him up.

Ironically, the first derby game of the 1923/24 season had the newspapers once more referring to a potential 9-1 hammering, which modestly finished in a 3-2 win for Sunderland at Roker Park. However, the reference carried some resonance at one point in the game as the home side scored three goals in five minutes. This resulted in some Black Cat fans singing "*1-2-3*" as they anticipated more goals.

Sunderland's team had had to be changed from the one that took the field in the previous game against Huddersfield Town (a 2-3 defeat) after, rather bizarrely, Warney Cresswell had tried to close a window in the team's dressing room during a communal bath and it caved in, shattering glass over one or two of the players. The South Shields man cut his shoulder and the injury required stitches; Jimmy Oakley took his place in defence.

It was the visitors who got off to the better start when, after seven minutes, Neil Harris struck a brilliant shot past Albert McInroy in the home goal, but then effectively lost the game in a catastrophic five-minute spell between the 19th and 24th minutes.

Billy Grimshaw, who had been signed from Cardiff City, was fed the ball by Buchan and delivered a beautiful cross, which was "breasted out" by Hampson straight to the foot of Paterson, who levelled the scores. Before Newcastle could regroup Sunderland were two goals ahead, courtesy of "Tricky" Hawes. The first came when Hawes took a pass from Parker and gently steered the ball to where Bradley had no chance of reaching it. One minute later Grimshaw once more sent the ball to the unmarked Hawes, and Hawes steered a cracking header past Bradley.

Newcastle were reeling and Sunderland sat back waiting for more goals to come. However, it was the visitors who weathered the storm and scored a second goal three minutes before the interval through Stan Seymour, who volleyed the ball into the net following a nice pass from Aitken. The visitors' cause wasn't helped by an injury to Cowan, who had to be carried off the field with a damaged knee just before half-time. He was patched up during the break and returned when the second half started but moved to outside-left, the customary place for injured players as there they could effectively do less harm.

One week later Sunderland did the double over Newcastle United by winning 2-0 at St James' Park in front of 50,000 people to become the first team to defeat the Magpies on Tyneside that season. It was something of a smash-and-grab raid as Newcastle controlled most of the game but couldn't do what matters most – score a goal. Both of Sunderland's efforts were scored by Paterson 25 minutes into each half.

Although the defeat was a disappointment to Newcastle they had a wonderful consolation in the FA Cup. They won the tournament on 26th April 1924 at Wembley Stadium, defeating Aston Villa 2-0, with two goals in the last seven minutes from Neil Harris and Stan Seymour, in front of 91,695 spectators. It had been a long journey for Newcastle en route to the final with, for example, four games required to defeat Derby County in one of the earlier rounds.

Although the regional Tyne–Wear League prize of four points went to Sunderland, the bigger national prize of the Football League crown would come tantalizingly close for the Wearsiders, but they lost out in the end by four points to Huddersfield Town, who won the First Division on goal average from Cardiff City.

The 45th league meeting between the two sides on 24th October 1924 produced the biggest crowd ever seen at Roker Park by some 6,000; the previous best had previously been in an English Cup tie against Burnley in 1920. As you would imagine there was a large crush inside the ground and many fans jumped over the barriers and sat along the cinder track to avoid the danger.

The game ended 1-1 with both goals coming in the first half, although the home side were handicapped by an injury to Billy Death.

Newspaper reports of the day indicated that it was a colourful and noisy crowd inside the stadium: *"This crowd contained all the elements associated with these encounters, the bell man, the bugler, the man with the rattle and even a black and white flag."*

The return game that season, in February, witnessed a Sunderland defeat, although this didn't come as a surprise given that Charlie Buchan was absent due to a leg injury that he had picked up in the Black Cats' previous game against Everton – a match in which the ace marksman scored twice.

Newcastle triumphed 2-0, with both goals coming in six second-half minutes through Tommy Urwin and Billy Cowan, although it could have been worse for the visitors had McInroy not been in inspired form in the Sunderland goal. He had given many fine displays that season and was being tipped as a future England goalkeeper.

The game on 17th October 1925 produced a 0-0 draw, only the fourth in the history of league meetings between the two sides. It was not, however, without controversy after Neil Harris had fairly shoulder charged the Sunderland custodian over the line – the referee failed to see this and waved play on.

By now Charlie Buchan had left Sunderland and his replacement, David Halliday, took little time in making an impact in a Tyne–Wear derby game, scoring in a 2-2 draw at Roker Park four months after the goalless draw. At the time of the game he was the First Division's leading goalscorer although it was Ted Harper of Blackburn Rovers who would have that accolade come the end of the campaign. The Black Cats had to twice come from behind in this game but the player that caught the eye was a young Newcastle defender named Ossie Park.

The following season saw Hughie Gallacher join Newcastle and make an immediate impact in the Magpies' side. So much so that after the 2-0 Sunderland win, a game in which Halliday once more scored for the home side, the media of the day reflected on Gallacher's absence and on how much they had missed his influence.

The first goal came from clever interplay on the Sunderland right wing, giving Halliday the easy task of steering the ball past Wilson.

The second was a brilliant snap shot by Death.

By the time the return game took place at St James' Park Newcastle were top of the First Division table and Sunderland were third. It was the 50th Tyne–Wear derby game and it was settled by a Hughie Gallacher goal after 32 minutes. An enormous crowd of 67,211 turned up to watch the spectacle, which smashed the previous best at St James' Park by over 4,000.

Newcastle's win put them firmly on course to win the league title, and this was duly wrapped up by a side that had been inspired by Gallacher. To put his influence into perspective the Magpies won the title by five points, and scored 96 goals in the season, including those in a 7-3 thrashing of Everton. They lost just one home game all season, winning 19 out of 21. Sunderland ended the table in third position, scoring 98 goals.

The two rivals met again the following season, with Newcastle aiming to defend their League Championship crown, and going into the game in second place in the table. United won the game at St James' Park 3-1 although the defeat could have been heavier for Sunderland had McDonald not missed a penalty for the home side after half an hour, shooting his spot kick wide. However, it was reported that he hadn't helped himself by having an argument with the Sunderland players as he prepared to take it. This was unfortunate for McDonald as he had given United a seventh-minute lead only to have it cancelled out three minutes later by an equalizer from Marshall.

In a game in which the home side were always superior, they pressed home that advantage with second-half goals from Seymour and McKay to take the points fairly comfortably.

For Sunderland this was a poor result to go with their other very average performances so far in the season. The defeat left Sunderland 19th in the First Division table. They would rally to 15th by the season's end but had a nail-biting final game in which they could have been relegated for the first time in their history. The season would end with seven teams on 39 points, including Sunderland, and bearing in mind that one of those teams, Portsmouth, was relegated on goal difference it emphasizes just how close the Black Cats came to demotion.

The return fixture at Roker Park saw Bobby Gurney, the legendary Sunderland striker, play in his first Tyne–Wear derby game, a game that would end 1-1. The home side went into the game having clawed themselves up to ninth place, with a 5-1 home win against Arsenal the previous week giving them confidence for the match against their Tyneside rivals. It was Sunderland who drew first blood when David Halliday scored after just 12 minutes of the first half. However, the goal was cancelled out by Tom McDonald towards the half-hour mark.

Newcastle ended the season in ninth place and could include in their 1927/28 season record some remarkable games, none more so than their 7-1 thrashing of Manchester United at Old Trafford – the highest away win of that season – and also a 7-5 home win against Aston Villa, the week before the Sunderland game – the highest scoring game of the campaign.

The 1927/28 First Division season was the one in which Dixie Dean, the ace Everton marksman, scored 60 league goals!

By now David Halliday had firmly established himself as a goalscorer to compare with almost any other, and in the following season he was the First Division's top scorer with a remarkable 43 goals. This helped Sunderland to an end-of-season fourth place.

A brace from Halliday helped Sunderland to a 5-2 thrashing of Newcastle United in October 1928 at Roker Park, over a relegation-haunted Magpie side who had new signing Jack Hill in their team, acquired from Burnley. With Hughie Gallacher away on international duty with Scotland the United fans went into the match with hopes low.

This feeling was well founded as the home side raced into a 3-0 lead after 25 minutes, and although Roddy McKenzie crashed a low drive home just after half-time to reduce the arrears, two goals in the final 10 minutes from McKay and Halliday completed the rout.

What hadn't helped Newcastle was a failure to play to the referee's whistle. Three times they had stopped to appeal for offside and three times the referee had waved play on.

The return game was a superb exhibition of football, with Newcastle winning 4-3. The man of the match was Hughie Gallacher, who scored twice. Quite remarkable for a game with seven goals was the fact that David Halliday failed to score even one of them!

A new ground record was broken when the official gate was given as 66,275, which was a superb effort considering that the Newcastle directors had raised admission prices for the fixture. The gates were closed half an hour before the advertised kick-off and the match therefore began 15 minutes earlier than planned.

The referee, Mr Watson from Nottingham, had refereed the 1925 FA Cup final between Sheffield United, the eventual winners, and Cardiff City, but he made no friends with the Sunderland supporters, denying them what they considered to be two stonewall penalties.

In an end-to-end game Newcastle took the lead three times, and were pegged back on each occasion. The Geordies' fourth goal, however, proved to be the killer blow.

Newcastle scored first on eight minutes when Urwin shot into the net following a good pass from McDonald. Sunderland levelled nine minutes later when Robinson crashed the ball home from close range after a centre from McLean.

Gallagher restored the home side's lead when he converted a 29th-minute penalty, but nine minutes before the interval McKay levelled the scores with a mighty drive. Burns got his fingertips to the ball but could not prevent it crashing against the underside of the bar and into the net.

United took the lead in the 60th minute when Allan turned

the ball into his own goal following a corner kick but 10 minutes later McLean scored a glorious equalizer. McKay had cleverly spreadeagled the defence and sent an astute pass to McLean who beat Maitland, cut in, and unleashed a stunning shot that rattled the netting. Gallagher scored Newcastle's winner about three minutes from the end with a real gem, as a centre from Lang went right across the goal, and the Scotsman, with a flick of his head, sent it through a very small gap and into the net.

Although Newcastle had won this game, overall it was a poor season for them, although they would rally to 10th place by the end of the campaign. Their season had included a 2-7 home thrashing by Burnley in April 1929.

In the final season of the decade the derby games commenced at Roker Park with a 1-0 win for the hosts. Yet again a ground record was broken when the attendance was given as 58,519.

Frustratingly, the ball was in the net five times during the game, however, only one of them counted, a 12th-minute effort by Sunderland's winger Gunson, following a pass by Allan. Magpie supporters contend that, in particular, an effort from Hughie Gallagher was onside, but despite vigorous protests the referee was so sure about his decision that he refused to consult a linesman.

The final encounter of the decade between the two sides took place at St James' Park and resulted in a 3-0 win for the home side, which came as a disappointment to the many Sunderland fans in attendance, as the team's defensive ranks had been strengthened by the arrival of Harold Shaw from Wolves for £6,000. Furthermore, considering that Gallacher was once more on international duty, it can be seen that such a reverse for the Black Cats meant it was a very poor day all round for them.

The result, however, did neither side many favours. Newcastle ended the game in 18th place whilst Sunderland all but propped up the league in 20th place. However, although the Black Cats rallied to finish ninth, Newcastle had a horrendous time, finishing just one point above relegation.

There were few bright spots in the season for either side: Sunderland could point to a 6-0 win at Anfield, the First Division's highest away win that season, and Newcastle had the consolation of a cup run that extended as far as the sixth round, where they met their match at Hull City.

FOOTBALL AT WAR

1930/31 to 1949/50

The Tyne–Wear derby games in the 1930s and 1940s were few and far between. In the potential 20 seasons of football only six of them produced competitive games between Newcastle United and Sunderland. This was due to two reasons. The first was United's relegation from the top flight in 1933/34 and the second was, of course, the Second World War.

During the Second World War the two clubs met on no fewer than 28 occasions in friendlies and in such competitions as the League War Cup, the North League and a Victory Game.

Many players guested for other teams during this period, dependent upon their whereabouts during National Service. Perhaps Sunderland's most famous and unusual wartime guest player was Jackie Milburn, the Newcastle United legend, who donned the red-and-white shirt on 24th March 1945 at Roker Park in a 2-2 draw with Gateshead, a friendly match that was watched by 3,200 people.

The first game between the two sides in the decade set the tone for what would follow for Newcastle a couple of seasons later, when Sunderland hammered United 5-0 at Roker Park.

Media reports indicated that Sunderland went about their work in the correct fashion but that Newcastle adopted the wrong methods and paid the price. The correct method, which gave Sunderland such a huge victory, was wide passing and progress on the wings. The wrong method was hugging the ball in the middle with short passes when the very nature of the ground, heavy, holding and sodden because of heavy rain, dictated the open game. Newcastle opened strongly because they made the ball do the work.

Sunderland's first goal came when Gurney picked up a pass on the left and swung across a centre that the unmarked Eden headed spectacularly into the net. Then, with the game 29 minutes old, Gurney allowed a centre from Eden to cross to the unmarked Connor, whose left-foot drive beat McInroy from close quarters.

After 71 minutes Eden gave Urwin an inside pass and he carried the ball close in without being challenged. Gurney did the trick when the ball came his way. Eight minutes later Connor fastened on to a ball which Naylor had deflected his way when attempting to clear a right-wing cross from Morris. Connor's left foot struck and the ball flashed past McInroy. Then, after 88 minutes, Eden got the ball from the left after a Connor–Gurney interchange and drove it wide of McInroy's left hand and into the net.

In the return game four months later Newcastle exacted revenge, although they had to wait until very late in the game for their two goals, which came – both from Harry Bedford – after 88 and 89 minutes.

If points had been awarded for pretty football and corner kicks Sunderland might have been near the top of the league instead of being near the bottom, and in this game Sunderland had just as many chances as Newcastle. However, it was recognized that flowery football didn't win football matches, and whereas United turned two chances into goals Sunderland frittered away their chances. For that reason United deserved to win, with Bedford's opportunism clinching the game for them and Eden's misses losing it for Sunderland.

It was noticeable that crowds were down significantly on the 1920s, partly because the number of coal miners in the northeast had dwindled to a third less than in previous seasons.

Neither Sunderland nor Newcastle did very much, league-wise, in 1930/31, but a bright spot, for once, came for Sunderland in the shape of the FA Cup; the Black Cats made it all the way to the semi-finals before being knocked out at Elland Road by Birmingham City.

The following season, for the first time since 1920, Newcastle succeeded in taking both points away from Roker Park. Their victory was well deserved but the 4-1 scoreline was more than United were entitled to on the balance of the play. Indeed, there was a spell during the second half when Sunderland threatened to give their fans the joy of seeing Newcastle's 3-0 interval lead wiped out as Joe Devine scored with a great shot from 25 yards, following a corner by Vinall after 53 minutes play.

This scoreline was a turnaround from barely one month previous when United had been thrashed 1-8 by Everton (the Toffees incidentally had also put nine past both Sheffield Wednesday and Leicester City on their way to winning the title and scoring 116 goals that season).

The return derby game in April saw Sunderland reciprocate Newcastle's Roker Park feat just over four months previously when they triumphed 2-1 at St James': the Black Cats' first league win on Tyneside since 1923. However, the home side had only themselves to blame when McDonald missed a penalty after 42 minutes; it came just 60 seconds after Benny Yorston had given the visitors the lead.

Having defeated Arsenal the previous week at Roker Park the win at St James' gave Sunderland the distinction of having beaten both of the FA Cup finalists within seven days. However, this defeat did not damage United's team morale as they triumphed at Wembley Stadium later on that month, with two goals from Jack Allen, one in each half.

It was reported by the *Sunderland Echo* after the match that, bizarrely, some 500 Sunderland supporters made the trip to Wembley to cheer on their arch-rivals in the final; indeed one of the fans was spotted carrying a lucky black cat into the ground.

As cup winners, Newcastle defeated Sunderland 2-0 at Roker Park the next time they met, with goals from Jack Allen and Tommy Lang.

In another tit-for-tat reprisal Sunderland defeated Newcastle at St James' Park with an early goal from Bobby Gurney and in doing so ended the proud home record of the Geordies, who had been undefeated at Gallowgate since early November. With it went United's chance of another league title.

The game was played in bright sunshine and on a hard playing surface, despite copious watering of the pitch for the last couple of days, which combined to handicap the players who, in addition to having difficulties controlling the ball, were also bothered by the heat. The journalists of the day decided that:

these factors all told against producing good football and can be held chiefly responsible for the very moderate standard on view. Sunderland deserved the victory though the margin between the teams was no more than the one goal scored represented.

Gurney's goal after five minutes was a fine individual effort that had its inception in a miskick by Fairhurst who put the centre-forward in possession. He was pressed to the touchline by Betton who then stumbled and fell, leaving Gurney unchallenged to dribble along the goal line and flash the ball between McInroy and the near post and into the far corner of the net.

It wasn't a good day for Sunderland's Jock McDougall, who was accidentally kicked in the face and needed stitches in his mouth after the game.

Although 12th in the league Sunderland could point to a relatively successful FA Cup campaign, which saw them reach the sixth round before being eliminated at Roker Park by Derby County in front of a 75,118-strong crowd, the largest ever attendance for a northeast football match.

The 1933/34 campaign was a disaster for Newcastle. They were relegated, along with Sheffield United, to the Second Division and wouldn't face Sunderland in a competitive game again until 1948/49 due in part, of course, to the Second World War.

Although Newcastle's form was obviously poor for most of the season this wasn't reflected in the Tyne–Wear encounters as both teams won their home games.

By the time the war ended, competitive football commenced, and Newcastle were promoted out of the Second Division (1947/48), the footballing maverick that was Len Shackleton had been and gone from Newcastle United.

Len was on Arsenal's books as an amateur and, initially thrilled to be chosen by Arsenal, his world nearly caved in when he was told by then manager George Allison that he would never make the grade.

At Bradford Park Avenue he was an instant hit and the Magpies took him to Tyneside where he enjoyed an eventful 18 months, including scoring six goals in a 13-0 mauling of Newport County. He played less than 60 games for United and it became evident that all was not well between Len and the Tyneside club. Subsequently it became known that offers would be considered for his services, which produced an auction, and it eventually came down to a straight choice between Bolton Wanderers or Sunderland, who were never shy at that time to put their hands in their pockets. In choosing the latter he achieved a British transfer record of £20,050 – the previous highest had been £50 less.

The Clown Prince of Soccer attracted massive crowds wherever he played, but an ankle injury in 1957 eventually brought a turbulent and eventful career to a close. All in all Len made 384 appearances for Sunderland and scored 101 goals.

After football he mapped out a career for himself as a journalist, first with the *Daily Express* and then the *Sunday People*. He lived in Cumbria with his wife Marjorie until his death on 27th November 2000.

He famously said that "even though I was born in Bradford and now live in Cumbria, I still consider the North East to be home. I love the place and the people are smashing. Newcastle people always tell me that I'm biased towards Sunderland but really I've nothing against Newcastle; I don't care who beats them."

A highly controversial statement from a highly controversial player, although perhaps this should be considered alongside the many run-ins he had with the St James' directors, culminating in Newcastle legend Joe Harvey's assessment that *"Newcastle would never win anything with him in the team."*

Whatever feelings Shackleton had towards Newcastle United it appears as though they were perhaps mutual.

Therefore there was some added spice when the two northeast giants met competitively for the first time in 14 years on 9th October 1948 at Roker Park, with Shackleton in the Sunderland side; a game in which, as fate would have it, Shack scored, to cancel out an eighth-minute goal by George Hair and end the match 1-1.

Shackleton, victim of an early tackle and many more within the first 10 minutes, was completely put off his usual game. He was in fact glad to get rid of the ball and instead of being his usual great individualist self he was in this match simply a ball distributor, although still the best Sunderland forward on view.

The northeast media reported that fans had started queuing at Roker Park the afternoon before the game, with three women from Birtley (a suburb of Gateshead) arriving dressed in the colours of both teams. A restaurant in Fawcett Street, Sunderland's main shopping thoroughfare, was decked out in red-and-white and black-and-white colours as it welcomed fans from both clubs for a pre-match scone and cup of tea.

The Tyne–Wear derby crowds were once more huge, over

51,000 watched this game, and this would be reflected in the postwar boom years when football recorded some of its highest ever gates. Indeed, until Sky television inspired the formation of the Premier League in the 1990s, the late 1940s and 1950s were perhaps the greatest known eras in English football.

In the return game at St James' Park, a typical blood-and-guts game that the home side won 2-1, the crowd was even bigger than the one seen on Wearside. This time some 58,250 watched an absorbing encounter.

Sunderland were starting to build what became known as the Bank of England Club, given its name due to the fact that the directors threw money around like confetti, regularly breaking transfer records in the process. Nevertheless, this strategy wouldn't bring them any trophies. Although the visitors could argue that they played the final 44 minutes of the game with 10 men after Walsh's injury, Newcastle deserved the points.

In this game, Bobby Mitchell made his competitive debut for Newcastle and, for the newly signed Chilean, Jorge (George) Robledo, it was a day to remember as he scored his first competitive goal for the Magpies, the winner after 64 minutes.

Sunderland had taken the lead through Ronnie Turnbull but Jackie Milburn scored an equalizer in the move that led to Walsh's ligament injury.

The 1948/49 season saw Newcastle United back on track and they finished an impressive fourth in the First Division, far better than big-spending Sunderland who could only muster eighth place. In the FA Cup neither side impressed.

It was a sombre meeting of the two sides when they met the next season at St James' Park where a one-minute silence was observed before the kick-off in memory of the former chairman of Sunderland AFC, Colonel Prior. Perhaps fittingly and diplomatically the game ended a draw, 2-2, a moral victory for the visitors who clawed their way back from two goals down, with effectively 10 men as Arthur Wright, who was injured, first of all reverted to the wing and then failed to appear in the second half.

The return game at Roker Park again ended 2-2, and was watched by an enormous crowd of 68,004 supporters, with many locked out. Again Newcastle had the upper hand but were twice pegged back by Sunderland goals, one of them from Shackleton.

At the end of the season and decade Sunderland boasted the First Division's top goalscorer, Dickie Davis, with 25 goals, but they were pipped to the league title by one point, with a disastrous home defeat by Manchester City in mid-April generally blamed as the root cause of this. Newcastle fared well, ending in fifth place, just two points behind Sunderland.

ST. JAMES' PARK, NEWCASTLE

A. D. BEASE, POST CARD SPECIALIST, NEWCASTLE-UPON-TYNE

NEWCASTLE UNITED V SUNDERLAND

Artist's impression of the Newcastle United v Sunderland encounter at St James' Park, 1901.

In September 1904 Sunderland travelled to St James' Park to play in a match for the benefit of the Officers and Men of the Fleet. Patriotic Tynesiders and Wearsiders turned out in their numbers; attendance reached 20,000.

Newcastle v. Sunderland. 1906. Won 4-2.

Newcastle United 4-2 Sunderland: Naisby, the Sunderland goalkeeper, saves a shot in the Tyne–Wear derby game at St James' Park, 1906.

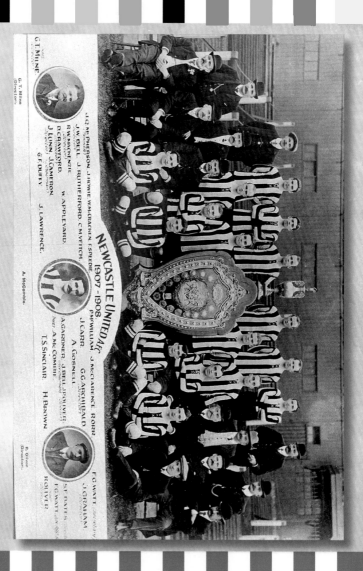

A superbly arranged photograph of United's squad and officials at the height of their Edwardian mastery in 1907. The trophies on show are the Football League title and the Sheriff of London Charity Shield the forerunner of the FA Charity Shield, now Community Shield.

NEWCASTLE UNITED A.F.C.
1907 - 1908.

J.Q.McPHERSON J.HOWIE W.McCRACKEN F.SPEEDIE P.McWILLIAM J.McCRACKEN R.ORR F.G.WATT (Secretary)
J.W.BELL J.RUTHERFORD C.MYETCH J.CARR G.G.ARCHIBALD J.GRAHAM
R.W.McKENZIE A.GOSNELL (Trainer)
D.CRAWFORD W.APPLEYARD A.GARDNER J.BELL J.OLIVER S.F.BATES
J.LUNN J.CAMERON (Asst. A.McCOMBIE) E.G.WATT (Jun. ASST.)
G.F.DUFFY J.LAWRENCE. T.S.SINCLAIR H.BROWN R.OLIVER

G.T.Milne A.McCOMBIE. R.Oliver
(Director) (Director)

RIGHT: George Holley, Sunderland's ace goalscorer and England centre-forward, was the bane of Newcastle United throughout his illustrious career, especially when he scored a hat-trick in the famous 9-1 win at St James' Park in December 1908.

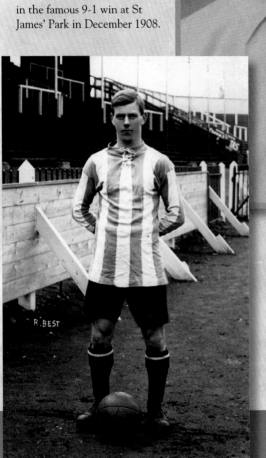

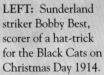

LEFT: Sunderland striker Bobby Best, scorer of a hat-trick for the Black Cats on Christmas Day 1914.

LEFT: Geordie legend Hughie Gallacher in his Newcastle United strip, circa 1925.

BELOW: Newcastle's victorious party of players and directors ready to head back to Tyneside with the FA Cup, 1932. Chairman James Lunn holds the trophy, flanked by Jimmy Nelson (left) and Jimmy Boyd (right).

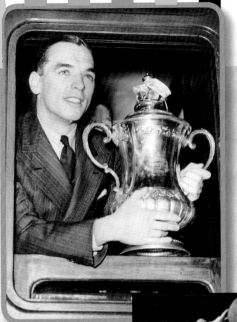

LEFT: Sunderland captain Raich Carter with the FA Cup trophy on his way back to Sunderland by train after his team had beaten Preston in the 1937 FA Cup final.

RIGHT: Midfield ace Sammy Weaver, one of United's stars of the Thirties, 8th March 1932. Weaver appeared for England and, in addition to his driving runs from midfield, he was famous for a prodigious long throw.

ABOVE: Len Shackleton, Newcastle United, circa 1946. Shackleton was one of the most talented footballers of the immediate post-war era. A supreme entertainer on the field, his wizardry as inside-forward and up front had defenders bamboozled. Shack remained at St James' Park for only a season and a half before making a big move to rivals Sunderland.

BELOW: Young Sunderland fans after their team beat Newcastle United to knock the Geordies out of the FA Cup, 3rd March 1956.

ABOVE: Jim Scott slams the ball past Jimmy Montgomery, in the Sunderland v Newcastle match, 31st August 1968.

LEFT: Ambulance men treat injured youngsters during the dramatic scenes before the start of the Sunderland v Newcastle United match at Roker Park, 31st August 1968.

Sunderland centre-forward Joe Baker has this close range shot saved by Newcastle keeper Ian McFaul as Ollie Burton tries to intercept. Newcastle United 3-0 Sunderland, November 1969.

A line of policemen and women control the Newcastle United fans at St James' Park in 1979 against Sunderland. Unfortunately the Tyne–Wear derby game has a reputation for crowd disorder going back decades. Here part of the huge police presence had their own mini-stools to enjoy the action!

League Cup, second round, second Leg, 6th September 1979: Jim Pearson holds his head in disbelief having missed the penalty that puts Sunderland through to the next round.

Sunderland v Newcastle United, Roker Park, 5th April 1980: Stan Cummins scores the only goal.

ABOVE: Former chief scout Charlie Ferguson and physiotherapist Johnny Watters (left) were given a testimonial match between the Sunderland 1973 FA Cup team and Newcastle 1974 FA Cup team, April 1986.

BELOW: Sunderland v Newcastle United, 13th May 1990: furious United players object to Hardyman's follow-up tackle on Burridge after a penalty miss at the Fulwell End that led to the Rokerman being sent off.

ABOVE: Marco Gabbiadini is chased by Newcastle's John Anderson and Ray Ranson.

BELOW: Newcastle United v Sunderland, 16th May 1990: Marco Gabbiadini celebrates having scored Sunderland's second goal.

Newcastle United legend Alan Shearer.

CUP FEVER!

1950/51 to 1959/60

The 1950s was a turbulent decade for Sunderland, and by the end of it they would be relegated for the first time in their history after an illegal payments scandal that rocked the football world. It would see the fall from grace of the only English team never to have played outside the top flight, and witness a nadir that would last on and off until the turn of the next century.

Whilst Wearside was caught up in *sine die* bans for directors and players alike (some subsequently overturned on appeal) Newcastle had other more promising exploits on their horizon, most famously some excellent FA Cup runs and wins.

The first derby matches of the 1950s took place within three days of each other in March 1951, with the first of them once more ending 2-2. A rare Joe Harvey goal after four minutes put Newcastle on track but two goals from Tommy Wright and Trevor Ford gave Sunderland a lead with minutes ticking down to the final whistle, until Jackie Milburn popped up in the 84th minute to level the affair.

Just 72 hours later on the Easter Monday Sunderland defeated Newcastle at Roker Park 2-1 with all the goals coming in the first half. This was Sunderland's first competitive win against Newcastle since the Magpies' relegation in 1934, technically 17 years, the longest winless streak in Tyne–Wear derby history.

Sunderland went ahead after 17 minutes when Shackleton pushed the ball forward to Ford. The latter seemed about to attempt a shot but only half hit the ball, which rolled to one side, allowing Kirtley to dash in and fire past Fairbrother. United's attempts to get on level terms looked feeble by comparison with Sunderland's polished moves, but a lot of credit for that goes to Hall, who strangled any attempt at birth by his tactic of keeping right on top of Milburn.

It was completely against the run of play when the equalizer came in the 28th minute: Mitchell scoring from a free-kick on the 18 yard line. The winger lobbed the ball over the defensive barrier and into the top corner of the net. Sunderland scored the winner six minutes later when Tommy Wright weaved his way into the middle and fed Ford with a pass as Corbett tackled. The centre-forward streaked clear of Brennan and shot past the advancing Fairbrother.

Whilst Sunderland ended the 1950/51 campaign in 12th place, Newcastle at one stage were on for a league and cup double. Although their league form subsequently went downhill it was different in the FA Cup where the Magpies went from strength to strength, defeating Blackpool in the final at Wembley Stadium 2-0, with Jackie Milburn scoring both goals within a five-minute spell early in the second half.

The last ever Christmas Day match between Newcastle and Sunderland 1951 saw Sunderland on the wrong end of a 1-4 thumping by their arch-rivals at Roker Park, with George Robledo notching a brace.

It was ironic that Newcastle should win only the second and last Tyne–Wear Christmas Day encounter by a margin of three clear goals, as the first time the fixture took place on this day – in 1914 – Sunderland had won by the same margin, triumphing 5-2.

The return game 24 hours later resulted in another 2-2 draw, and was remembered for a wonderful display by Sunderland's Trevor Ford. The centre-forward's courage, superlative moments from Shackleton and, for Newcastle, the skill of the Robledo brothers were high notes of the two games.

Newcastle's line-up was unchanged from the Christmas Day clash but Sunderland played Hedley instead of Stelling against

Mitchell and dropped Kirtley for Arthur Wright at inside-left, with Shackleton switching to the right.

As at Roker Sunderland were the fastest into their stride and after 41 minutes they went ahead. Ford was clean through when Brennan trod on the ball and McSeveney centred for Bingham to hit McMichael's legs on the goal line. Robinson turned a Foulkes' header round the post and tenacious Ford then beat Brennan, with Bingham netting from a McSeveney pass.

On resuming, Walker hit the ball hard just inside the box, striking Hall on the arm. It looked a harsh penalty award but Milburn made telling use of it. Five minutes later Simpson's goal kick hit Ford on the 18 yard line. The ball rebounded a couple of yards, but Ford was on to it like a flash and netted with a low shot.

Arthur Wright let two chances slip but then Milburn, missing the ball in a crowded penalty area, found time to half turn as the ball bounced and his left-foot shot beat the unsighted Robinson to level the game.

Newcastle again won the FA Cup on 3rd May 1952 when they defeated Arsenal at Wembley with a goal six minutes from time scored by the Chilean George Robledo, in a match refereed by Arthur Ellis. The South American was also the First Division's top goalscorer with 33 goals.

The following season the shades of night were falling fast at St James' Park on a first Newcastle win of the season when, nine minutes from time, Tommy Wright, Sunderland's right-winger, tore through the middle to shoot into the top corner of the net from 30 yards and gain the Black Cats a 2-2 draw. It was probably a fitting end to the first Tyne–Wear evening derby on 10th September 1952.

Typically it was Shackleton who declared himself fit the day before the match and who helped Sunderland take the lead in a game in which he was rarely in the picture. Shackleton wore the No. 8 shirt and Watson the No. 10, but for almost all the game they were in switched positions. However, when Sunderland got a corner on the right, Shackleton went over and landed the kick left of middle. The ball bounced but Watson flicked it past Casey and, as it bounced again, with Batty moving in, Watson jabbed it into the net.

A Jackie Stelling own goal was followed by Reg Davies putting Newcastle ahead in the 73rd minute. The crowd of 60,727 could see that tackling and challenging were difficult, with the strong wind adding to the difficulties of the players. The trainers were kept busy; Crowe seemed to be under a handicap for most of the second half, Milburn finished with ankle trouble and Watson was out for some time on the cinder track late in the game. There were many other knocks and before the interval Hall was taking goal kicks for the Sunderland goalkeeper Threadgold.

Both teams had two outstanding players. Brennan did his best to captain United to victory and right-winger Walker made a sparkling return. Watson at inside-forward for Sunderland was the player of the game and Arthur Wright added many touches of class distribution. One more player on either side came near to honours. Reg Davies for the home side and the Roker pivot, Fred Hall.

At Roker Park seven days later the return Tyne–Wear derby did a lot to make up for the many disappointing postwar clashes between Newcastle and Sunderland. It was a game that had everything: a contest in style, all-out battling with no quarter asked or given, and the occasional touch of artistry by individual players. Newcastle won 2-0 in front of nearly 60,000 people but to be honest they were flattered by the margin and result. Territorially Sunderland dominated the game throughout and should have piled on a big score. The Sunderland attack won nine corners to Newcastle's one. However, the Newcastle attack was much more methodical.

It was George Robledo who opened the scoring in the 20th minute when a Davies shot had beaten Threadgold and hit the bar. The centre-forward found himself in the right position to meet the rebound with his head and put the ball into an empty net.

Seven minutes later came the only black spot of the match, with the United centre-forward again being the dominant figure. Robledo was involved in an incident with Reynolds and, to a storm of boos, he was cautioned by the referee while the Sunderland winger was receiving attention.

Newcastle's second and deciding goal came on 75 minutes. Davies got the ball into the Sunderland net but was well offside, but in United's next raid it was in again and this time it counted. Robledo dispossessed Hedley and from his pass Davies fired against the foot of the post. Threadgold got a hand to the ball but could not prevent it rolling along the line for Mitchell to score the goal that put the contest out of Sunderland's reach.

During 1953 it was reported that Sunderland had tried to buy Jackie Milburn from Newcastle to boost their forward options and although the Magpie star was keen to join up with his friend Shackleton the Gallowgate directors turned the move down flat.

The 1953/54 season was a pretty miserable one for the northeast's big two clubs, one in which Newcastle would end the season in 15th place, whilst Sunderland finished 18th, just three places above relegated Middlesbrough.

Sunderland went into the first derby match of the 1954/55 season in third place, and the 4-2 win at Roker Park against a Newcastle side languishing in 12th place saw the Black Cats go top.

It was a sweltering October day as the teams took to the field before a huge attendance of 66,654 to watch thrill-a-second football in which Sunderland's full-strength side was solid and competent. Although talk of honours for the side was premature, the media of the day indicated that *"if this eleven can be kept together as often as possible the club should be close when April arrives"*.

The United backs were instantly harassed by Sunderland's wingers, however, the Geordies had two of the game's best players in Mitchell and Crowe. Mitchell gave Hedley a roasting and had Milburn been able to head in his opportunities in the first quarter hour – one a wonderful opening that needed only a flick of the head – matters might have been different.

The best players for Sunderland were the wingers. Bingham was brilliant and went into the game having scored four goals in the last two matches. However, both Fraser, the Sunderland custodian, Shackleton and Broadis were pale shadows of themselves in this encounter. Nevertheless, taken over the 90 minutes it was a fine team performance and a thrilling match.

Sunderland led 2-0 at half-time then increased their lead to 3-1 and 4-1. Three of the six goals were excellent: Millburn's lovely angled drive which even Fraser scarcely saw, Bingham's header from Elliott's cross and Ken Chisholm's run in from a shrewd forward pass to net.

Sunderland's first two goals were opportunist as Purdon rolled the ball over the line from a few yards out from an acute angle, despite that fact he looked safely covered, and Bingham netted a spectacular 25-yard left-footed lob. Aitken was unluckily penalized for hands as White drove into a crowded penalty area, which gave Mitchell the chance to drive in a goal from the spot to end the scoring after 67 minutes.

The return game in February 1955 saw Sunderland win again, this time at St James' in front of another bumper crowd of over 60,000. Although there was obvious disappointment from the Magpies they were consoled by the fact that they were in the middle of an epic FA Cup run that would see them win the trophy for the sixth and, so far, last time. In fact Sunderland also made it to the semi-final and, having been kept apart from their Tyneside rivals in the draw, they succumbed to a defeat by Manchester City at Villa Park. Newcastle would defeat York City in a replay, ironically at Roker Park, before defeating the Black Cats' conquerors at

Wembley in the final 3-1. Jackie Milburn scored after 45 seconds, the quickest ever Wembley Cup final goal until 1997.

In the league game Newcastle were only a few inches away from victory instead of defeat in a rousing Gallowgate derby. Had Keeble, only five yards from goal, been able to stoop two inches lower, he might have opened the scoring after five minutes from a short pass from the right by Hannah. But the home captain could not get his head sufficiently low to touch the ball, which bounced short for Fraser to palm clear.

In the 20th minute Keeble climbed high to a Milburn cross but was again two inches too high, meeting the ball at eye level, and away it went over the bar. Finally, with the score 1-1 midway through the second half it looked as if it would be third time lucky for Keeble, but another header from Mitchell's centre struck Fraser on the knees as the keeper moved along the line and it bounced to safety.

That virtually cooked Newcastle's goose, for in the later stages the main thrills were a fine save by Batty on the line from Elliott, a lovely Fleming header that just missed and an injury-time header from Hedley's free-kick that settled the issue.

Cannonball Fleming opened score when Sunderland's right-winger Kemp, a Stockton lad recruited from out of the Northern League, and playing just his third senior game, headed down an Elliott cross for Fleming to score from six yards. In the second half Jackie Millburn's goal came after about six seconds of play, when the ball moved from Keeble to Broadis to Hannah, who was fouled. Scoular's free-kick went to Milburn, who scored.

Despite this crucial win Sunderland would end the season in fourth place in the First Division table, four points from the top in a league won by Chelsea, the only time they won the league title until the arrival of Roman Abramovich. Newcastle ended eighth to make it a reasonably good campaign for the two clubs, given their heroic exploits in the FA Cup.

The following season league games were played on consecutive days over the Christmas period, the first on the Boxing Day. At Roker Park Newcastle thrashed Sunderland 6-1 to record their best ever win on Wearside and equal the devastating defeat handed to the Black Cats by their Tyneside neighbours in 1920.

Three players notched twice for Newcastle in a match watched by over 55,000 people, with around 15,000 Magpie fans making the short trip to Wearside.

Four magnificently headed goals were among the sparkling gems of a game in which United's Keeble was, of course, to the fore in this "heady" (excuse the pun) atmosphere. He rocketed in number one in the second minute from a free-kick by Casey after Anderson had bundled Mitchell. Fraser scarcely saw the ball again when Keeble headed in from Millburn's corner to notch number four in the 28th minute.

Milburn, who came back to form, never used his head better than when rising to flick into the net a forward chip by Davies in the 67th minute. That made the score 5-1 after Fleming had faced an Elliott free-kick and, meeting the ball full on, rammed it home in the 48th minute.

Other Newcastle scorers included Jackie Milburn who, in the 14th minute, took a Davies pass, dummied McDonald in the corner of the box, and slipped it home. In the 18th minute, Curry swung his foot close in to finish off a forward pass from Mitchell. Then, in the 81st minute the ball came over from Milburn to Mitchell in front of the posts and Curry was there again to drive hard into the net.

Ironically the corner count at the end of the game showed that Sunderland had nine and Newcastle five, perhaps emphasizing just how deadly the Newcastle strike force had been on the day; everything they hit went in.

Twenty-four hours later Newcastle United had a double over

Sunderland when they again triumphed, this time 3-1, to give United their first Christmas treble since 1932/33 (they also hammered Preston North End 5-0).

The crowd were intrigued by Sunderland's four forward changes, which included Bill Holden, signed the previous day from Burnley, and the introduction of right-winger Kemp. Shackleton switched from right to left and Billy Elliott went to inside-left.

United fans were shocked when Holden scored after five minutes as a result of a move that started when Elliott brought the ball past Scoular in a sliding tackle – Holden netted when Kemp's shot was blocked.

For Newcastle's first goal Daniel kicked away White's shot in the 53rd minute, only for the winger to prod the ball forward again. Keeble headed on and with Davies distracting Fraser, the ball came back off a post, allowing Keeble to tear in and slam it into the net. Aitken was off the field having a head wound attended to when Milburn scored Newcastle's second two minutes later, and later Allan went outside-left with Elliott as wing-half and Shackleton as an inside-forward. For Newcastle Scoular was at half pace for most of the game following a wrench of his right knee, although this didn't prevent the home side scoring again when Len White wrapped the game up right on the final whistle.

The final result could have been different had Fleming not missed a sitter, which would have made it 2-0, although in the end the victory saw Newcastle move up to sixth in the table, above Sunderland on goal average.

Although Sunderland may well have been down in the dumps at two defeats in two days from their nearest and dearest they were provided a platform for revenge a couple of months later when the two clubs were drawn together in the sixth round of the FA Cup. This time, however, the outcome would be different, as Sunderland moved into the FA Cup semi-final for the second consecutive year when they won 2-0, with both goals coming from Bill Holden.

He headed the first goal four minutes before the interval with Paterson, his marker, right beside him. Ronnie Simpson, the home goalkeeper, advanced some three yards but then heard the ball whistle past his ear into the net. Anxious to keep the ball in play with Holden in attendance, Paterson let in the Roker player for number two in the 83rd minute.

Sunderland lost the subsequent semi-final game at Hillsborough to Birmingham City 0-3.

A crowd of 61,474 paid record receipts of £9,600, which topped the recent Gallowgate record established against Stoke City. The extra 6p charged in the paddock helped in this respect.

The season ended with both of the teams adrift in mid-table.

In the topsy-turvy world of the Tyne–Wear derby Newcastle turned the tables the next time they met, in August 1956, with a goal three minutes from time, giving United a victory they scarcely deserved, and concluding the 81st derby match. During the game, and taking everything into consideration, there is no doubt that Sunderland were the better team. United's sole advantage, and it proved to be the decisive one, was the conversion of scoring chances.

At virtually any stage of the second half up to that late goal, a harassed and tormented Newcastle side would have been mighty glad to settle for a draw, whereas Sunderland's only concern seemed to be that they could not turn their territorial advantage into a winning margin. Making light of a thunderstorm accompanied by torrential rain that left water standing on the pitch, the Sunderland forwards swarmed round the United goal for half an hour after the interval and yet only had one goal and a host of near misses to show for their efforts.

Six minutes before half-time, just as the rain started, United went in front, Davies putting over a diagonal centre and Milburn diving to beat Bollands with a header from about 15 yards. Sunderland's great fight back started with the best move of the match. Almost immediately after the second-half kick-off, Hannigan, Anderson, Shackleton and Fleming interpassed brilliantly, only for the centre-forward to fire just past the post.

The equalizer came in the 54th minute when Crowe made an inaccurate pass; Shackleton beat Scoular to it and made ground before beating Simpson all the way with a wonderful shot from 25 yards. At this point Shackleton was inspired. He made another excellent chance for Fleming, who pulled his shot wide, and then tried another long-range shot himself, only to see it hit the bar despite Simpson being helpless.

As the end approached it looked like a draw, until, with three minutes to go, the ball went to Mitchell, who hit it straight into the middle. There, Davies met it with a downward header that bounced into the far corner of the net, with Bollands caught out of position.

The return game, three days before Christmas, not only saw Newcastle once more thrash Sunderland, this time 6-2, but Alex Tait become the first United player ever to score a hat-trick in a Tyne–Wear derby game. Another notable statistic was that it was the first time that any team had won four successive Tyne–Wear League derby encounters.

Newcastle United's young lions tore the star-studded Sunderland side apart in a match that thrilled and entertained 27,727 spectators who braved the dismal conditions. With the ground shrouded in deep pea-soup-like fog and gloom it was a wonder that the match was played at all, and on a treacherously waterlogged surface it was even more remarkable that the players were able to produce such a good game.

The visibility was so poor that thousands of spectators were kept waiting outside the ground until 35 minutes before kick-off time when the referee, H Webb of Leeds, decided that it would be possible to start. Even then, with the puny Gallowgate floodlights struggling to pierce the mist, few in the crowd or on the field thought that the game would be finished. For the record this was the first time that a Tyne–Wear derby game had been played under floodlights.

But before the match had run a quarter of its course, the chief worry of Sunderland supporters and players alike must have been that it would *not* be abandoned. The plain truth was that in the whole 90 minutes Sunderland were only occasionally in the picture as an attacking force. Their forward line which, with Shackleton and Revie playing together for the first time, looked on paper to be the strongest club attack in the country, was a miserable failure.

United stormed into it right from the kick-off and there were good efforts from Davies and Casey even before they took the lead in the seventh minute. Chiefly responsible for the goal was Casey – in a terrific shot which Bollands pushed away at full length. It was a magnificent save but not good enough because White came steaming in to crash the ball into the empty net.

In the 21st minute United scored again. A White corner was helped on by Davies and the ball rebounded from a defender to Tait, who quickly turned to fire into the net through a packed goalmouth. It became 3-0 in the 37th minute after a move begun by a long diagonal pass from Davies to White. From the outside-right's centre, Tait put a close-range header straight at Bollands: the goalkeeper could not hold it and the ball rolled to the foot of the post where Tait coolly applied the finishing touch.

For the remainder of the half Sunderland's forwards managed to produce some decent play and after forcing three corners in quick succession they got a goal back in the 41st minute. Anderson started the move with a cross pass to Elliott, who sent the ball forward for Shackleton. The inside-left pulled it back from the left of goal and Fleming beat Simpson with a low drive.

Though the fog began to thicken again at the interval nothing could dim the sparkle of United's forwards and with the second half only 11 minutes old Tait completed his hat-trick with a splendidly taken goal. A forward pass from Curry found the young centre-forward unmarked, but not far inside Sunderland's half. Tait carried the ball forward quickly and with defenders converging on him, calmly planted it past the advancing Bollands. A couple of long-range shots from Shackleton was all Sunderland could make in reply until they reduced their arrears in the 64th minute, Fleming scoring with a powerful shot after being put through by Revie.

Any hopes Sunderland may have had of a dramatic rally were, however, quickly snuffed out. Six minutes later Casey gave Bollands no chance from the penalty spot after Daniel had been penalized for a foul on Tait. After 72 minutes United scored their sixth, with Davies crashing one in from 15 yards after White had run almost to the byeline and then pulled the ball back.

The season ended with neither side having impressed in the First Division. In fact Sunderland, now embroiled in an illegal payments scandal, were lucky to be still in the division, having ended the season 20th. The Roker club were starting to look doomed despite having spent so much money that they had become known as the Bank of England Club.

The season of 1957/58 would be a watershed one for them.

Sunderland were in relegation trouble right from the off and an early season meeting of the two clubs at Roker Park on 21st September, which Sunderland won 2-0, saw the Black Cats 21st in the First Division table before the game (in a 22-team league).

Few people expected a struggling team like Sunderland to outplay their neighbours in such fashion as this but in the end the score flattered United, not Sunderland. Much the better side throughout, Sunderland squandered numerous scoring chances.

United scarcely made one clear-cut scoring chance in the game and Fraser, in the home goal, had no more than a couple of shots to save. The quality of the football was never high, but what constructive play there was came almost exclusively from Sunderland. The victory also ended their run of four defeats at the hands of United.

Considering that it had absorbed over an inch of rain in the previous 12 hours, the pitch cut up surprisingly little during the game, but with drizzle falling throughout the ball was greasy and the turf treacherous. On this tricky surface Sunderland were quicker into their stride and only an extraordinary miss by O'Neill prevented Sunderland from taking a six-minute lead when Mitchell fumbled a ball from Anderson.

Two minutes from the interval Sunderland at last got off the mark when the Magpie goalkeeper Mitchell just beat Fleming to a through pass from Anderson, but the ball ran loose to Revie who coolly lobbed it in before the goalkeeper could recover. United opened the second half much more promisingly, but seven minutes after the interval Sunderland increased their lead with their first real attack of the half. After a move with Bingham on the right, Fleming put the ball across and Grainger headed in just inside the far post, with Mitchell, probably unsighted, diving too late.

The last Tyne–Wear derby game of the 1950s took place on 1st February 1958, and ended 2-2.

Most people expected Newcastle to be carved up and most people were proved wrong for a host of reasons, most importantly the fact that they underestimated the team's fighting quality. Added to this was the power and ideas of Davies and Mitchell who had Sunderland battered and reeling in that fantastic first half.

Newcastle's goals, like several near goals, were well engineered. First Davies robbed Anderson and angled a short pass for Tait to score from eight yards after 23 minutes. Then, eight minutes before half-time, the ball was switched via Davies to Eastham to Tait for Curry to head cleanly home from Tait's cross to the far post. At the interval the game looked to be over but Sunderland fought back in a second half where Newcastle lost their grip on the stamina-sapping pitch and almost apologetically crept back into the game through Elliott's penalty and O'Neill's header.

It was touch and go for both sides to the end, with Franks almost snatching a winner with a couple of minutes to play. If he had there could have been few grumbles.

Sunderland would ultimately be relegated on the last day of the season for the first time in their history, despite defeating Portsmouth 2-0 at Fratton Park. Leicester City, their rivals for the relegation spot, defeated Birmingham City 1-0 and stayed up, which was ironic given that the Foxes' manager was none other than former 1920s ace Sunderland marksman David Halliday.

Newcastle United, however, were little better, and only escaped demotion on goal difference. They had the same number of points as Sunderland: 32.

BACK IN THE BIG TIME

1960/61 to 1969/70

With Newcastle United relegated at the end of the 1960/61 season, the next time the two teams would meet competitively would be in the Second Division. There were also four non-competitive games, two in the Cock o' the North competition and two testimonial matches, one of which Sunderland lost heavily, 2-6, at Roker Park.

What was noticeable from the match reports of the day was that crowd disorder was now prevalent, with pitch invasions not uncommon, almost a throwback to the late 19th and early 20th century.

In front of 53,991 spectators at St James' Park the first derby of the 1960s was a thriller that would end 2-2; it was summed up by the media as follows:

In their time these two teams have played before bigger Derby crowds and produced better football. But for atmosphere and excitement there has been nothing quite so gripping as the furious battle that these keen rivals fought out to the last gasp at St James Park. It could have gone either way but on the whole the 2-2 score line did justice to the occasion. It would have been tough on either side to go down after giving everything in a game that provided peak soccer entertainment.

Close marking and quick, fierce tackling had both attacks well pinned down from the start and there was still nothing in it in until the 17th minute when McGuigan hit a long ball out to the left to find Wilson clear of Cecil Irwin. Wilson cut in before making his centre and Len White side-footed his shot at a wide angle that had Wakeham diving vainly for a ball just out of his reach. Then Harry Hooper beat three opponents in a 70-yard dash before laying the ball on the centre for Clough to claim an equalizer in the 66th minute. This was the signal for hundreds of Sunderland youngsters to swarm on to the field and the game was held up until police had cleared it. Within two minutes United were ahead again. McGuigan, on the 18 yard line, pulled down a pass from Allchurch to hit a low drive through McNab's legs. Wakeham was unsighted and had no chance as the ball flashed wide of his right hand. United's younger element expressed their delight too with a pitch invasion. In an attempt to prevent any further invasions, an announcement revealing that the referee had said he would abandon the game if any more invasions took place was made over the tannoy.

With only five minutes left to play Hooper repeated his earlier run, again drawing Hollins to the near post before centring. Again Clough was there to tangle with Keith to get the goal. United were badly shaken especially as Hooper, now roaming in search of a winning goal, looked as though he had found it when racing through from a deep centre-forward position. Defenders converged on him and Hollins was racing from his line as Hooper approached the penalty area. However, his left-foot shot flashed inches wide of the right-hand post.

The 86th Tyne–Wear derby was played at Roker Park on 21st April 1962; it was a game in which the hosts won 3-0, with two goals from George Herd. The signing of the Scotsman from Clyde caused something of a rift between the Black Cats and the Magpies, with the latter unhappy at missing out on his signature after having travelled to Glasgow and agreed a fee with his club on 25th April 1961. They then returned to the northeast and read in the *Evening Chronicle* the next night that he had signed for their rivals.

In the Newcastle game Sunderland gave everything they had in a game that was said to rank among the greatest of Tyne–Wear derby matches. For 57,666 spectators who stuck it out in continual rain there was an endless sequence of thrills and incidents spiced with brilliant soccer at a cracking pace.

The game took its decisive turn in the 19th minute when Herd, already in full stride before the pass was made, chased a ball from Clough through the inside-left position and went right up to Hollins before pushing the ball past him.

Though the score stood at 1-0 for the next 57 minutes the game was always running against United. With the exception of two fine efforts from Allchurch early in the second half they were never in it. Clough missed two good chances and McPheat saw a close-range drive strike McMichael and rebound clear. Then came the goal that virtually settled it. Anderson measured a brilliant pass over McMichael's head and Hooper, taking it in his stride, was clear in a flash. Hooper closed the range before making his shot and when Hollins palmed the ball along the line McPheat dashed in to push it into the empty goal. On a dry day it would have been Hooper's goal, for the ball stuck in the mud on the line. Herd produced the final touch eight minutes from the end, stumbling out of a tackle to take the ball to the 18 yard line before beating Hollins with a right-foot drive placed with such power and precision that the goalkeeper could not get anywhere near it.

Barrie Thomas, Newcastle's instinctive goalscorer, cut a sad figure as he fought unsuccessfully to force a single chance and was outplayed by Charlie Hurley. Indeed, both of United's expensive wingers were well taken care of by Ashurst and Irwin who were both in peak form; this was one of their finest games as a pair. Montgomery, Sunderland's 18-year-old wonder goalkeeper, played superbly well, marshalling his defence and generally demonstrating why he was so highly rated and seen to have such an exceptionally safe pair of hands.

Sunderland had gone into the game with the Magpies as genuine promotion contenders but would agonizingly miss out on promotion to Leyton Orient, who went up into the First Division along with Liverpool. The hammer blow for Sunderland was at the Vetch Field in the final game of the season where, having led through a Brian Clough goal, they let that advantage slip and an equalizer from Swansea saw the Black Cats miss promotion by one point. Hard to take given that Sunderland had lost just once at home all season.

However, such bad luck would befall Sunderland again before they were eventually promoted.

The following season the first game in the series took place on Tyneside in front of over 60,000 fans, with an estimated 15,000 locked outside. Both teams were riding high in the league and the game provided a treat for those lucky enough to gain entrance.

With Charlie Hurley out injured for Sunderland they were obviously weakened but it didn't show and, slightly against the run of play, the visitors scored after 30 minutes when Brian Clough met a Jimmy Davison cross to slot the ball home from a couple of yards out. Newcastle then stepped up the pressure and were rewarded with an equalizer just three minutes before half-time when their inside-forward, Jimmy Kerray, shot from 10 yards. Although kicked rather weakly, the ball ricocheted off Stan Anderson and deflected past an already committed Montgomery.

Despite the fact that there were no more goals in the second half there was a scare for Newcastle when their inside-forward, Dave Hilley, went down under a clumsy challenge from Jimmy McNab; however, the referee waved play on.

If the first derby of the season had been a good and eventful game the return at Roker Park was less so. Although the game was affected by a severe frost that required a pitch inspection by the local referee, Kevin Howley from Middlesbrough, right from the kick-off the visitors set their stall out very defensively and, pleased with their day's work, trooped off at the end of the game with a point gained from a 0-0 draw. Sunderland fans went home feeling short-changed, having seen their favourites control almost the entire game.

Although Newcastle faded towards the end of the season and finished seventh in the league table, Sunderland took the field for their final match of the season knowing that a draw against Chelsea, who lay third, would be enough to see them promoted. However, they lost at Roker Park in front of a crowd of nearly 50,000, and were pipped two promotion places by the Londoners, on goal difference, and Stoke City, who were top with 53 points. Another campaign dogged by bad luck for the Black Cats.

The 1963/64 campaign would be the season where the bad luck stopped for Sunderland and they would finally win promotion, coming second in the table to an emerging Leeds United side. For Newcastle it would be an average affair where they rarely threatened much and ended well off the pace, a full 16 points behind their arch-rivals.

The Black Cats were already second in the table when the two teams met at Roker Park in front of another bumper crowd in October 1963, and with Newcastle in eighth place it was a game that the home side were expected to win.

Interestingly, Stan Anderson, a stalwart of the Sunderland team since the early 1950s, was left out and, unknown to Roker fans, wouldn't play another game for the club again. After 447 first-team appearances he would leave and, ironically, sign for Newcastle United, becoming one of the very few players to move in that direction.

The Geordies took an early and surprise lead after 14 minutes when Alan Suddick's cross was converted by Colin Taylor, only his fourth goal for the club since his move from Walsall. Roker Park was stunned into silence.

The home side then upped the pace but found the Newcastle defence in frugal mood and it took a goal from left-back Len Ashurst to equalize with just two minutes of the half remaining; the Sunderland skipper Charlie Hurley was off the field receiving stitches in a head wound following a clash with the Magpies' Barrie Thomas. Lennie the Lion's goal was a beauty as he cracked home a 25-yard free-kick on what was his 200th appearance for the club.

Hurley led the team out for the second half, much to the relief of the Sunderland fans, but he had little to do as the home side piled on the pressure. Indeed, with time running out it looked as though Newcastle would leave Wearside with a precious point against all the odds. However, with just nine minutes remaining George Mulhall sent in a lovely cross shot which George Herd steered past Hollins in the United goal to give the Black Cats a 2-1 win.

The fixture five months later at St James' was notable for two things, a surprise 1-0 Newcastle United win and also some misinformation that led to a crowd of only 27,341 attending the match when at least double that was expected. This came about due to the atrocious weather conditions that day as the rain bucketed down. It was erroneously reported in the local media that the match was off due to a waterlogged pitch and many people didn't bother leaving their homes as bus and train services were cancelled.

In front of what was a paltry crowd for the time the two teams battled for supremacy on a quagmire of a field in a game where Sunderland went into the fixture top of the Second Division.

Once more Jimmy Montgomery was in inspired form, saving miraculously from Willie Penman; however, there was little he could do to prevent the one goal that did go past him, a penalty, after Charlie Hurley had handballed inside the penalty area. Ron McGarry stepped up and although Monty dived the right way the kick was too powerful and nestled nicely in the back of the net.

Although United had much the better of the second half they could not force home a second and decisive goal. Nevertheless, a 1-0 win sufficed to give the Black Cats the jitters as the promotion run-in commenced.

However, the red and whites would prevail come May, and United would have to wait another year for promotion.

The two teams would recommence hostilities two seasons later on 3rd January 1966 at Roker Park in front of nearly 55,000 people. An interesting precurser to that game had been the Brian Clough testimonial match that had been played two months earlier on Wearside to mark the end of the prolific striker's career through injury. However, the result between a Sunderland and Newcastle Select XI didn't quite go the way Clough would have hoped as the Tyneside team trounced the Black Cats 6-2. Nearly 32,000 spectators turned up to wish Ol' Big Head farewell.

In the league encounter, however, Sunderland had much the better of the fixture and ended up winning 2-0 with second-half goals from two of their Scots players, George Herd and John O'Hare.

In that game Charlie Hurley was injured after 39 minutes and had to be helped from the field. Mike Hellawell came on as a substitute and became the very first person to do so in a Tyne–Wear derby game (substitutes were only permitted from the 1965/66 season onwards).

The game had been originally planned for 27th December 1965 but a heavy frost and an unprotected pitch had resulted not only in a postponement but in some criticism for the Wearside club.

A curious incident was reported before the match took place when, on the morning of the rearranged game, the groundsman at Roker Park had opened the stadium only to find that the goalposts had been painted black and white, presumably by some mischievous Newcastle fans that had scaled the walls of the Fulwell End the previous night. Needless to say there was some quick whitewash applied and all was well with the world again from a Sunderland perspective come kick-off time!

By now, of course, both teams were back in the First Division but neither were doing particularly well; indeed the form of both sides would be poor for the duration of the campaign with Newcastle ending the season 15th and Sunderland 19th, just three points from relegation.

At St James' Park in March 1966 the Magpies repaid the favour and defeated Sunderland 2-0 with a brace from Alan Suddick. With Pop Robson injured Joe Harvey, the United manager, took the unusual step of naming Ollie Burton, normally a wing-half, as centre-forward. Burton was a stalwart for United for nine seasons and had the distinction of being the first-ever substitute to be used by them when he came on for the injured Trevor Hockey in the 2-0 victory at home to Northampton Town earlier on that season.

However, it was to be a bad day for Burton when, following a clash with the Sunderland hard man Charlie Hurley, he was stretchered off after only 20 minutes and immediately substituted by Peter Noble. This was, ironically, the first time Newcastle had ever used a substitute in a Tyne–Wear derby game; it was later revealed that the injury was so serious that Burton would take no further part in the season. Although he would play for Newcastle again, like Clough his career would be prematurely ended in 1973 due to a knee injury and he would play his last game for the Geordies in January 1972.

United having been thrashed 0-6 the week before the derby game by Blackpool, Joe Harvey decided to splash out on a striker for the 93rd league game with Sunderland on 29th October 1966. Wyn "the Leap" Davies duly arrived from Bolton Wanderers and made his debut for the Magpies, but he was unable to make much impact as the Black Cats ran out convincing 3-0 winners in front of 57,643 supporters.

The irony of the Davies signing is that the fee, some £80,000, was £5,000 more than the two clubs had agreed 12 months previously, but that deal had fallen through at the last minute. Perhaps it demonstrated the desperation at St James' Park as they went into the derby game in 17th position (slipping to 20th after the defeat). Bizarrely, in order to keep the deal from the press, the meeting between Newcastle and Davies had taken place at a sheet metal firm owned by a Bolton fan.

George Mulhall opened the scoring for the visitors after just seven minutes when an innocuous cross evaded Gordon Marshall in the Magpies goal and nestled nicely into the far corner of the net. It got worse for Newcastle just four minutes before half-time when a Len Ashurst cross found Neil Martin and, unchallenged, he headed the ball home to give the visitors what was to prove an unassailable lead.

With 10 minutes remaining George Mulhall created an opening for John O'Hare, who slotted the ball home for number three, so ending the scoring.

The return game, some four months later at Roker Park, saw Sunderland achieve a rare seasonal double over their Tyneside rivals: the sixth and, to date, last time that this has been achieved by the Black Cats.

In advance of the game, teams made up of Newcastle and Sunderland supporters met for an inter supporters' club game at Seaburn that the Roker fans won 4-1. It was a doubly painful day for a Magpie fan, Davie Urwin, who broke his leg and had to be taken to the Sunderland Royal Hospital, thus missing the game.

The supporters' game was a good omen for the Black Cats as they won 3-0, with the match being staged just one week before the first of three absorbing FA Cup fifth-round ties that the Roker side would play – although they would ultimately lose against Leeds United.

Newcastle went into the Tyne–Wear derby game in deep, deep

league trouble and lay 21st in the table. Sunderland weren't much better in 15th but were still the overwhelming favourites.

The first half was a poor spectacle but the game came alive in the second period when a young Bobby Kerr scored 11 minutes into the half, intercepting a John McNamee back pass to glance a header past Marshall in the Magpie goal. It was McNamee's ninth game following his previous December move from Edinburgh side Hibernian.

Kerr then scored his second goal 18 minutes later, slotting the ball home having intercepted a George Mulhall cross shot. With two minutes to go George Mulhall ended the scoring to give the home side a convincing win.

The 1966/67 campaign was a poor one for both sides but more so for the Magpies who ended 20th, third bottom, only escaping relegation to the Second Division by four points. For them, it was a season to forget.

Prior to the 95th derby game, which was to be played at St James' Park, it was revealed that Sunderland were interested in signing the Leeds United Scottish Under-23 international Eddie Gray; however, the Yorkshire side's Don Revie was adamant that he wasn't for sale at any price.

Sunderland went into the game at Gallowgate in poor form, and a 1-2 defeat at the hands of their bitter rivals hardly helped to ease the pressure on the Roker boss Ian McColl.

The gates were closed long before kick-off, with an estimated 5,000 people locked outside.

Newcastle took the lead after 23 minutes when Wyn Davies scored following a lovely cross from Albert Bennett, although Montgomery in the Sunderland goal complained that he had been fouled by the Welshman.

Bennett, from Chester-le-Street in County Durham, had the distinction of being named as Newcastle's first ever substitute in the game against Nottingham Forest on 21st August 1965, although he was not used. He was also the player rugby-tackled by Emlyn Hughes, which gave the Liverpool player his nickname "Crazy Horse".

Surprisingly Sunderland, playing in their all-red strip, drew level four minutes later through Colin Suggett, who scored a beauty, cracking home a low shot from 30 yards that beat the goalkeeper all ends up.

It was Bennett himself who scored the winner with 20 minutes to go when he hit another beauty, a 20-yard "banana shot", that screamed into the net with Monty helpless.

The return game came just four days later on 30th December 1967 and ended in a 3-3 draw. The game saw Ian Porterfield, newly signed from Raith Rovers, make his league debut for a side that went into the game in 19th position in the First Division table. The Scot had been spotted during a mining disaster fund-raiser between Sunderland and a Fife Select XI on 25th September 1967, and impressed in the all-star side's 4-2 victory.

Colin Suggett, celebrating his 19th birthday was Sunderland's man of the match as he scored two of his side's three goals in the space of four first-half minutes.

However, it was Newcastle who opened the scoring after 13 minutes when Wyn Davies was clearly brought down inside the penalty box by Charlie Hurley, and Ollie Burton converted the spot kick.

It was then that Suggett turned the game on its head to give the home side a 2-1 lead at the interval.

Just two minutes into the second half Bruce Stuckey made Sunderland's lead seem unassailable at 3-1 when he crashed home a cracking shot to up the noise from the Roker Roar.

With nothing to lose United poured forward and their perseverance was rewarded with 20 minutes to go when they were awarded a second penalty after Dave Elliott was upended by Ralph Brand. Burton once more converted the penalty to set up a grandstand finish.

With Charlie Hurley having gone off injured Sunderland gradually began to look desperate as they tried to hang on to the lead by all means possible. Inevitably, and with three minutes to go, the Geordies snatched a point when McNamee leapt high to meet an Iley corner and crashed a header past Monty, swinging on the crossbar in celebration.

The 1967/68 campaign ended better for Newcastle who finished 10th in the league, whilst Sunderland were five places lower. In the FA Cup neither side prospered to any great degree.

The 1968/69 campaign was memorable for Newcastle United. Although they didn't make much of an impression in the First Division, finishing 10th in the league table, they went on an epic European adventure that led them all the way to the European Inter-Cities Cup final and a two-legged 6-2 aggregate victory over the crack Hungarian outfit Újpest Dózsa. It was the first time that United had competed in a recognized European trophy and it had been a pulsating journey that had seen them defeat teams such as Setúbal from Portugal and, infamously, meet Glasgow Rangers in a home tie that was riddled with crowd trouble both on and off the pitch.

Consequently, the Tyne–Wear derby games were overshadowed, particularly as both ended 1-1.

However, of concern to Sunderland AFC was their perilous financial situation, and with crowds dwindling the club was fast approaching a transitional stage that would see stalwart and club legend Charlie Hurley leave on a free transfer at the end of the campaign – one that had seen Sunderland receive a record league thrashing 0-8 by West Ham United at Upton Park in October 1968.

Therefore, Sunderland went into the 1969/70 campaign in poor shape, and it got no better for the club as they scored a mere 30 goals all season in games that were watched by an average crowd of little more than 21,000.

With Newcastle on the up the Black Cats were put to the sword in the first league derby game at St James' Park on 8th November 1969, losing by a 0-3 margin. Willie McFaul in the home goal had little to do all afternoon whilst Montgomery, the visiting custodian, was busy, pulling off save after save in an attempt to keep the red and whites in the game. However, there was little he could do to stop Keith Dyson scoring twice and Wyn Davies notching the other goal.

After the game there was fighting between both sets of fans in and around Central railway station, with the Sunderland supporters' train having several carriage windows put out.

The last derby match of the decade was the 100th Tyne–Wear League derby game and was played at Roker Park in front of nearly 52,000 fans.

Sunderland went into the game in relegation trouble, and would be demoted at the end of the season along with Sheffield Wednesday, whilst Newcastle lay sixth in the First Division.

Jimmy Montgomery was once more magnificent for Sunderland and stood between the Black Cats and a hiding. However, he was powerless to stop "Jinky" Jimmy Smith from giving the Magpies a 51st-minute lead, and although Bobby Park equalized, one point wasn't really much good to Sunderland.

There was some controversy about the Sunderland goal as Park's shot had hit the underside of the bar and come out, only to be nodded in by Dennis Tueart, but Sunderland manager Alan Brown gave the goal to Park.

Due to Montgomery's outstanding performance for Sunderland that season he was included in the provisional England squad that was due to travel to Mexico for the 1970 World Cup, although subsequently he would be omitted from the final group. Given Peter Bonetti's shambolic display when England were eventually knocked out by West Germany in Leon this was perhaps a mistake by the national selectors.

However, the fact that the 100th derby game ended 1-1 wasn't the main talking point. Once more crowd violence made the headlines, with the *Daily Mirror* reporting prior to the game that a "Skinhead Soccer Armoury Is Seized". This was in reference to a discovery by an inquisitive policeman of a stash of weapons that had been thrown over the wall of the Fulwell End by Sunderland soccer thugs, to be used before, during and after the fixture with Newcastle.

The armoury consisted of more than 50 weapons, including bottles, knives, spikes, carving forks, scissors, chisels, hammer heads and lead piping. The scheme had become unstuck because of the vigilance of a police Panda car driver who became suspicious when he saw a group of about 12 youths bunched by the wall. He pulled up and the youths, who were wearing Sunderland red-and-white scarves, ran off. The policeman then searched inside the ground and found the sackful of weapons.

Chief Superintendent Ronald Kell, Sunderland's divisional commander, said later: *"It was really a horrific collection. In the wrong hand they could have caused considerable damage and injury. The youths must have known that they would be searched at the turnstiles and so decided to try to smuggle their armoury in."*

Another police officer said: *"The oddest item was a wooden potato masher, which had been carved to inflict damage when thrown."*

Other weapons, including studded belts and bicycle chains, were collected at the turnstiles when police "frisked" youths as they entered the stadium.

Before the match, teenaged Newcastle United fans invaded a supermarket. When they could not get into a cafe upstairs, they began hurling tins of food about. Five windows were broken. Furthermore, a group of 300 Magpie fans threw bricks and smashed 30 house and shop windows on the way to the game; they also overturned a car and fought running battles with the Sunderland supporters in the streets outside.

The 1969/70 season was fraught for Sunderland and, fighting for their First Division lives, they entered the final day of the season knowing that a home win over fifth-placed Liverpool would see them leapfrog Crystal Palace to safety. Rather typically they lost 0-1 and went down.

Meanwhile, back on Tyneside, a steady season for United saw them end the table in seventh position, having participated in the Inter-Cities Fairs Cup once more. They reached the quarter-finals in the latter before being eliminated on away goals by Anderlecht from Belgium.

STRANGERS

1970/71 to 1979/80

By now Sunderland, in particular, were a club in trouble. As they were seemingly unable to stay in the top flight, during the 1970s there were only eight competitive games played between the Black Cats and the Magpies, a mere two of them in the top flight. Indeed, other than testimonials and meaningless minor cup games such as the Texaco Cup the pair didn't play each other competitively until 1976.

By that time Sunderland had, of course and famously, defied the odds to win the 1973 FA Cup final, defeating Leeds United, one of Europe's most feared sides, in a memorable Wembley final. The Magpies almost replicated this but lost to the machine that was Liverpool the following year 0-3. They tried again, this time in the 1976 League Cup final but succumbed again, this time to Manchester City, who were inspired by a bicycle kick goal from an ex-Sunderland player, Dennis Tueart.

It was during the mid- to late 1970s that the term "FTM" came to be used by Sunderland fans with reference to their Tyneside rivals. Whilst officially this meant "Follow the Mackems" it was widely known that it was really a derogatory term in relation to the "Mags". However, in time the Newcastle fans reciprocated and came up with an equally uncomplimentary term for their Mackem counterparts – "SMB" (Sad Mackem Bastards) – although this acronym was subsequently translated as "Sexy Mackem Bastards" by the Sunderland fans, underlining once more the tit for tat belligerence and at times juvenility that afflicts this near 400-year-old social saga.

The 1970s were also significant in that, on 13th March 1976, a local newspaper, the *Northern Echo*, reported that workmen at Boldon, the site of the famous battle, had uncovered the remains of three skeletons buried deep in solid limestone as they dug a sewer. The bodies were subsequently identified as those of soldiers who had fought on that far-off day. It was a poignant reminder of what started the rivalry in earnest.

The first competitive football game between the two teams took place two days after Christmas Day in 1976 at St James' Park. Backed by up to 10,000 fans housed in the Gallowgate End Sunderland tried their best, but a lack of class told from a club propping up the First Division table and destined to go down, albeit with an end-of-season fight.

Sunderland were under the cosh right from the off and the only surprise at half-time was that the score was a mere 1-0 to Newcastle; the goal was scored four minutes before half-time by Paul Cannell and was a lovely header that flashed past Barry Siddall in the visiting goal.

Newcastle once more dominated the second half but again they had to wait until the dying embers of the half to double their lead, which they duly did after 83 minutes when Alan Kennedy crashed home a shot from an acute angle.

The return game at Roker Park some four months later was played out in a completely different atmosphere to the first. With Sunderland woken from their slumber a fight was now on to avoid relegation, a fight that, unlike the one in December, looked like a winnable one. Having thrashed Middlesbrough, West Bromwich Albion and West Ham United, scoring 16 goals in the process, the Black Cats had lost just two of the previous 10 games, whilst Newcastle went into the fixture in fourth place.

A packed Roker Park greeted the teams on a sunny Good Friday afternoon, and a rather subdued first half came alive with just four minutes of it remaining when the Sunderland midfield schemer Kevin Arnott crashed a beautiful shot past Mahoney in the United goal. It got worse for the visitors 10 minutes into the second period when Bob Lee pounced on a loose ball when Mahoney could do no more than parry a Mel Holden effort.

At 0-2 Newcastle looked dead and buried, however, with just one defeat in the previous 10 games they too were high on confidence and pulled back the arrears after 70 minutes when Paul Cannell scored in similar circumstances to Lee, and when a Micky Burns shot was only parried by Siddall, the Sunderland custodian, allowing the Magpie striker to slam home the rebound.

By now it was all Newcastle, and although the home side piled on the pressure they couldn't force a way through until, with just four minutes remaining, Tommy Craig blasted home from 25 yards.

Although a draw was a fair result it was generally agreed that had the game gone on much longer the visitors may well have snatched it.

The season would end with Newcastle in a UEFA Cup position, but for Sunderland it was relegation after last-gasp heartache at Goodison Park where, defeated by Everton, they prayed for a miracle in the game at Highfield Road where Bristol City were visiting Coventry City. A quite outrageous draw was played out between the two teams in circumstances that have subsequently been questioned and an FA inquiry was demanded by Sunderland, but to no avail. They went down.

If Sunderland thought that they wouldn't face Newcastle for a while they were wrong as, inexplicably, the Magpies folded during the 1977/78 season and were relegated with just 22 points from 42 games. Therefore the two rivals met each other at Roker Park in October 1978 in a game whose backdrop of English football violence saw an orgy of destruction that took place both on the Newcastle fans' way to the ground from Tyneside, and in and around the ground as kick-off approached.

Such violence had years still to run before action was taken to clean up the game, and, both home and abroad, the good name of English football was being dragged through the mud in front of an increasingly disgusted world.

In fact the fear of violence was all-pervading and in this encounter the crowd was more than 10,000 down on the official capacity of Roker Park.

Both teams went into the game in reasonably good shape with Newcastle sixth and Sunderland just outside the top 10. Indeed it took only 13 minutes for United to demonstrate why they were slight favourites as Peter Withe scored a header from a Nigel Walker free-kick, with the Sunderland central defender Jeff Clarke caught in no man's land.

Sunderland thought they had evened the score after 35 minutes but an Alan Brown effort was disallowed after he was judged to have impeded the visiting custodian, Hardwick.

At half-time it was 0-1 with all to play for.

Not long into the second period Newcastle could have sewn the game up when a lovely move down the flanks saw Nigel Walker, the Magpies' man of the match, send in a lovely cross, which was met beautifully by John Connelly. His effort beat Siddall but somehow was kept out by Bob Lee of all people; he headed it clear from under the crossbar.

A significant moment occurred after an hour's play when Roy Greenwood was introduced and Gordon Chisholm substituted. It took the former Hull City player just 14 minutes to make his mark when a move instigated by the Sunderland full-back Joe Bolton was passed on to Gary Rowell and then Mick Docherty. The latter's shot on goal was parried by Steve Hardwick and Greenwood smacked home the loose ball.

On the field it had been a good game but off it there were a total of 100 arrests or ejections from the stadium.

Sunderland's first league victory at St James' Park since 1966 on 24th February 1979 has taken on almost folklore proportions in the 31 years since the event. The match will, of course, always be synonymous with Gary Rowell. His influence on the game was massive as his hat-trick plunged Tyneside into mourning.

The Black Cats scored after only six minutes when a Jeff Clarke free-kick was sent goalwards, Gordon Chisholm headed the ball into a ruck of players and, with a swing of his boot, Rowell somehow forced the ball through. The Leazes End, packed with red and whites, erupted.

However, early play did not go all Sunderland's way as Siddall had to be smart to deny Peter Withe on two occasions, the first necessitating a tip over the bar as the Magpie striker met a Nigel Walker cross brilliantly. Bird was booked for a professional foul on Rowell as the Roker maestro started to prompt and probe his way through the black-and-white defence. On 25 minutes Blackley lost out in the heart of the midfield and Kevin Arnott lobbed a beautiful pass into the path of Seaham's finest, who drove the ball to the left of Hardwick from outside the box and into the net for number two. At half-time Sunderland led, but early in the second half, on 50 minutes, the Magpies gave themselves hope.

Henderson brought down Connelly, and with Newcastle man of the match Walker flighting a pinpoint cross, Connelly rose high to smack the ball past Siddall.

However, Sunderland's third goal was the killer from which the home side never recovered. On 60 minutes Rostron wriggled his way through the middle, sending Henderson free and Mitchell could only watch in horror as his clumsy challenge resulted in a penalty, which Rowell tucked away with his usual aplomb to become only the fifth Sunderland player in Tyne–Wear history to score a hat-trick in a derby game. With just 18 minutes to go it was Rowell who reached the byeline and crossed, allowing Wayne Entwistle to head in at the far post, completing a wonderful individual performance.

As a postscript to this match it became clear in the aftermath that there had been large-scale crowd disorder prior to kick-off. In what has become known as the Battle of Bath Lane the Sunderland supporters who travelled by train fought their Newcastle counterparts on the journey to St James' Park, and through the streets of the city, particularly in the Westgate Road area.

The last season of the decade, 1979/80, saw the Tyne–Wear rivals meet on no fewer than four occasions, the first two games being in the Football League Cup. Both games would end 2-2; however, a dramatic penalty shoot-out at St James' Park, following on from the Roker Park game, saw the Black Cats through to the third round.

A talking point of the game on Wearside was the size of the attendance, just 27,658 – the lowest for a competitive Tyne–Wear derby game at Roker Park since 1930/31. Although prices had been increased for the game the League Cup has never been a very popular tournament with clubs, and with a triple whammy of an all-ticket occasion plus a fourth factor – the threat once more of crowd trouble – it was understandable that attendance was down.

In the first leg Sunderland took an early 19th-minute lead through their midfielder Wilf Rostron, who headed home a Gary Rowell cross from 12 yards out. As the game wore on it looked like that would be the end of the scoring until a 10-minute spell late in that period sealed the draw.

After 73 minutes a mazy run by the home striker Alan Brown resulted in the Newcastle keeper, Hardwick, bringing him down. Bryan "Pop" Robson fired home the spot kick. However, as in previous Roker Park fixtures between the two sides Newcastle refused to give in and they set up a nail-biting finish when Ian Davies scored his first goal for the Magpies with 14 minutes left.

Then, seven minutes later, it was Peter Cartwright, a 71st-minute substitute for Gary Nicholson, the John Connelly understudy, who earned the visitors a draw with a firm header following an indirect Mick Martin free-kick.

The second leg at Gallowgate again drew a poor crowd of just over 30,000. With the Sunderland fans housed in the Leazes End an absorbing game didn't come to life until the 74th minute.

Sunderland took the lead through Alan Brown – a header that sent the visiting contingent wild – but in a game of contrasting emotions for them Newcastle scored twice in a devastating six-minute spell to set up an anxious finish. The first by new recruit Stuart Boam was a header after 80 minutes and the second yet another header, this time from the ex-Blyth Spartans man, Alan Shoulder, with just six minutes remaining.

However, with the home fans reminding the referee that time was up Boam turned from hero to villain as he allowed Alan Brown to outpace him and smash the ball home to end the game tied at 2-2.

Extra-time brought no more goals, but plenty of excitement, and the game would be decided by Association football's very own Russian roulette, the penalty shoot-out.

Sunderland went first and scored all seven of their penalties: Robson, Rostron, Buckley, Ashurst, Whitworth, Chisholm and Brown being, in turn, the Johnny-on-the-spot for the visitors. Once Newcastle had scored their first five through Shoulder, Withe, Martin, Davies and Brownlie, the game had, of course, become sudden death. Although Barton scored the home side's sixth spot kick there was stunned silence from the Geordies when Jim Pearson missed. He never played another game for Newcastle after that!

Newcastle were out.

Although not reported at the time this was the second time that Sunderland had technically scored nine goals at St James' Park in one match, following on from the never-to-be-forgotten game in 1908.

Still smarting from this defeat the Geordies had the chance for revenge at St James' on New Year's Day 1980 and took it, defeating Sunderland 3-1 in front of a much healthier gate of 38,322. The home side went into the game top of the table although Sunderland were close behind them in fifth place, just four points behind their rivals.

Although United were clear favourites a tricky surface evened things up and it was the away side who coped better early on. The Black Cats duly took a surprise lead after 25 minutes when Brownlie in the home defence misjudged a long punt out of goal by Chris Turner, the Sunderland goalkeeper, and Stan Cummins nipped in to steer the ball home past Steve Hardwick, off a post.

With seven minutes of the first half remaining Peter Cartwright again scored for Newcastle against Sunderland, chipping a glorious goal from 20 yards.

It didn't take long for Newcastle to sew up the game in the second half when, after 56 minutes, Tommy Cassidy latched on to a poor clearance from Sunderland's Argentine midfielder, Claudio Marangoni, and lashed the ball home from 25 yards. Worse followed for the red and whites just two minutes later when Shaun Elliott handled the ball in the box: Alan Shoulder stepped up to fire the spot kick home and seal the points for the home side.

The last game of the decade was played out at Roker Park and it produced a win of 1-0 for Sunderland. In hindsight the Roker faithful should probably have made more of the win as it would be nearly 30 years before Sunderland would defeat the Magpies again on home soil. Another interesting statistic is that it would be the last attendance of over 30,000 ever at Roker Park for a Tyne–Wear derby game, as crowds in general plummeted and the ground became increasingly unfit for purpose.

Newcastle went into the game having won just one of their last eight league games and were on the crest of a slump. By the end of the match the two teams would swap places in the league table. Guttingly for the Geordies they would fade away badly and, after a promising start to the campaign, they ended ninth while Sunderland would be promoted as runners-up to Leicester City.

In a competitive game there were few goal-scoring opportunities in the first half but a decisive moment in the fixture came after 73 minutes when Stan Cummins slid in at the far post to score and send Roker Park wild with delight (visiting supporters excepted, of course!).

Although Sunderland ended the decade on a high it was Newcastle who had undoubtedly, league-wise, enjoyed a better time.

YO-YO

1980/81 to 1989/90

If people thought that the 1970s had produced nowhere near enough Tyne–Wear derby games then goodness knows what they thought of the 1980s as the two teams met each other just four times in the league: twice in the First Division and twice in the Second Division. There was no real precedent for this as the last time this had happened there had been a good excuse – the Second World War.

There were a couple of friendly games right at the beginning of the decade, and for Sunderland the period did bring about one of the all-time classic wins from their perspective – the 1990 play-off game at St James' Park.

Nevertheless, as both teams yo-yoed around the divisions, the two clubs became even more strangers to each other than the previous decade, with Sunderland suffering the humiliation of relegation to the Third Division of the Football League in the first season of their new chairman Bob Murray's reign. Unfortunately for Murray relegation was to be a haunting presence during his tenure as the club were demoted no fewer than five times in 20 years.

It was fully five years into the decade before Newcastle and Sunderland met competitively, at St James' Park on New Year's Day 1985, a game in which the visitors fancied their chances due to a spate of injuries within the home ranks, including that suffered by Chris Waddle.

However, the game was an unmitigated disaster for Sunderland as not only did Peter Beardsley score a hat-trick, only the second ever by a Magpie player in a Tyne–Wear derby game, but they suffered the ignominy of Howard Gayle and Gary Bennett being sent off – something that sadly produced racist chanting from the home supporters against the two black players as they left the field.

Racist chanting at this time was extremely prevalent in England and it would eventually lead the FA and PFA to support the "Kick Racism Out of Football" movement that would have Gary Bennett as one of its main backers.

The consequence, thankfully, has been a huge reduction in racist incidents in and around English football grounds, including those in the northeast, assisted by the influx of African footballers into the Premier League, many of which have found a temporary and welcoming home with both Sunderland and Newcastle United.

The return game in the April was a less eventful affair on the pitch, finishing 0-0, but off it there was trouble as a group of Newcastle fans gained access to the Fulwell End, which was packed with home supporters. Inevitably crowd trouble followed and the "infiltrators" had to be escorted from the home end along the side of the Clock Stand where they were pelted with coins and insults and into the Roker End where the away fans were situated.

A main feature of this season as far as Sunderland AFC was concerned was the way in which it utterly fell apart as the campaign wore on. Although they were never very high up in the Football League First Division table at any point they got themselves embroiled in a Milk Cup (League Cup) campaign that saw them all the way to a Wembley final where they were defeated by Norwich City. Distracted from the league they then lost game after game and ended up relegated.

Newcastle and Sunderland would not meet again until the 1989/90 season in the Second Division, following United's demotion in 1988/89 as the top flight's bottom club. Although three of the matches, all fairly mundane draws, would again have more headlines due to off-the-field events, the final game, a play-off decider, produced fireworks wherever you looked. It wasn't a game for anyone neutral, who would have wondered exactly what they had walked into.

The first league encounter was at Roker Park and, uncommonly for the time, it was staged on a Sunday with a noon kick-off, due to police fears of crowd disorder. As always that fear was well founded but, fortunately, the goalless draw may have ensured some fans were too bored to fight.

The return game on Tyneside was more exciting, with Marco Gabbiadini, the darling of the Sunderland crowd, giving the visitors the lead just after half-time. This was, however, cancelled out, with a little more than 10 minutes remaining, by Mark McGhee.

The draw was enough to cement Newcastle in sixth place in the league table, with Sunderland one place higher. Intriguingly, as fate would have it, the former ended third with the latter sixth when the normal league season finished, putting them in direct competition for a play-off final place at Wembley.

The first leg would be played at Roker Park with the second at St James'. What followed was the explosion of a Tyne–Wear incendiary device.

At Roker Park the first leg of what was officially the Football League Second Division play-off semi-final was played out in front of a paltry crowd of 26,641 with 4,000 away fans in attendance. However, the atmosphere was still poison. On the pitch the game itself wasn't much better but it exploded into life in the very last minute when a clumsy tackle by Newcastle's Mark Stimson felled Gabbiadini inside the penalty area. It was an obvious penalty but this didn't stop the visiting players remonstrating with the referee. Paul Hardyman, the Sunderland full-back, took the penalty and looked on horrified as it was saved by John Burridge, the Newcastle custodian; it was the ninth penalty failure by a Sunderland player against Newcastle. By way of demonstrating his frustration

Hardyman did no more than run up and kick Burridge near the head.

Despite the referee inevitably and rightly dismissing Hardyman for this display of violence, all hell broke out on the pitch with both sets of players involving themselves in an ugly scuffle.

This then prompted the supporters into action and, with the perimeter fencing at Roker having been removed due to the distressing scenes at Hillsborough on 15th April 1989, supporters, mainly of Sunderland, encroached on the playing area.

Although the police and stewards bravely and efficiently sorted the trouble out the events on and off the field that day undoubtedly left tensions running high; they were still high during the second leg, which was played at St James' Park three days later on 16th May 1990. Effectively this was a winner-takes-all game for the right to meet either Swindon Town or Blackburn Rovers at Wembley for a play-off final game that would lead to the top flight.

There was plenty at stake!

Supporters entering the ground could immediately sense the tension in the air; proverbially you could have cut it with a knife. No neutral person, other than a complete masochist, would have enjoyed a "game" (the term loosely used) that neatly encapsulated a 400-year war between two cities.

Before the game both sets of supporters and players were warned to stay calm; furthermore, there were over 500 police officers on duty to ensure that the events passed off peacefully. However, both the warning and the deterrent failed to prevent some of the worst scenes on a British football ground in years.

Although Newcastle went into the game as favourites Sunderland had a great away record, having won 10 games on their travels, with six draws. United's home record was, however, daunting – a very impressive 17 wins and four draws from 23 games.

Within minutes of the game starting it became pretty evident that Sunderland were right up for the game but Newcastle just couldn't settle and their aimless high balls into the box were swallowed up by the Sunderland defence, most noticeably Gary Bennett, a rock in the Black Cats' central defence. With Warren Hawke, Sunderland's young left-winger, always a menace it was hardly surprising when the visitors opened the scoring after 13 minutes as Eric Gates coolly slotted the ball home at the Gallowgate End.

Tensions rose during the second half as the home attacks amounted to nothing, but the flame that lit the fuse to an explosion of dynamite ignited with just five minutes of the match remaining.

It was Hawke, Sunderland's young gun, who started a left-wing move, playing a delicious ball to the feet of Gabbiadini. The latter then played a one-two with man-of-the-match Eric Gates, who returned a precise pass which Marco slid home, right in front of the travelling Sunderland fans in the Leazes End.

As the Sunderland fans erupted in delight the home fans, incensed at the prospect of humiliation by their age-old rivals on their own patch, invaded the pitch in their hundreds, an obvious attempt to have the game stopped. As the police fought running battles with United fans and as the Sunderland fans taunted them mercilessly, George Courtney, the local referee from Spennymoor, County Durham, took the players from the field.

Although the first pitch invasion was quelled, a second erupted, and the players were off the field for almost 20 minutes. Courtney famously told the players that he would stay at the ground all night if necessary to complete the fixture.

The atmosphere that greeted the players when they returned was poison, no other word for it, and the remainder of the fixture was played out. As the final whistle approached some of the players made sure they were near the tunnel area and immediately sprinted to the safety of the dressing rooms when the game was finally brought to a halt.

In all 66 supporters, mainly from Newcastle, were arrested, with a dozen police officers and a dozen supporters injured.

While this was a night of shame for Newcastle United FC, the fans of Sunderland rejoiced at the humiliation heaped on their near neighbours. A bittersweet trip to Wembley awaited the Black Cats, while Tyneside reflected on what might have been.

At the time Jim Smith was manager of Newcastle United and in his subsequent autobiography, *Bald Eagle: The Jim Smith Story*, he revealed that *"the passion and antagonism between Tyne and Wear has been going on for years and we really felt its hot blast when we played Sunderland in the play offs. That one game with Sunderland was a make or break for the season, and, of course, it was made doubly worse for our fans in that it was the loathed red and whites who turned the knife. I think they could forgive us anything, except losing to Sunderland."*

Sunderland would subsequently travel to Wembley and once more they would lose at the home of football, due to an own goal, to a Swindon side that were ironically being investigated for illegal payments to players under a former regime. Found guilty of this misdemeanour the Wiltshire side's win counted for nothing and Sunderland, in a curious twist of fate, took their place in the top flight once again.

It was bittersweet for Sunderland AFC to think that some 30 years after an illegal payments scandal that saw the implosion of their club, they would benefit from another such event.

What goes around inevitably comes around.

THE ENTERTAINERS

1990/91 to 1999/2000

Football was changing in England and a new phenomenon was about to overtake the game in the shape of what was initially called the Premiership. Although great claims were made as to the advantages of the league with respect to the England national team (promises that never materialized), the formation of what would morph into the FA Premier League took, some would say, world league football on to a new level. Giant revenue streams emerged from its commercial contracts, most significantly with television, and radically moved the game from a moribund sport, with 19th-century facilities and appalling crowd behaviour associated with both violence and racial intolerance, into one of the most envied and copied templates that reached not only far-flung football fields but sports such as cricket with the formation of an Indian Premier League.

In doing so, however, there were complaints that a working-class sport was being sanitized to such a degree that it made the game much less appealing to some – although with attendances about to boom, the money men took no notice.

As a result of the Premiership what was Football League Second Division would become Football League First Division, and this change filtered down to what was the Fourth Division to create a headache for many football statisticians, with various novel slants put on previous footballing league trophy wins.

Neither Sunderland nor Newcastle United would compete in the inaugural Premiership season in 1992/93.

Almost forgotten, however, was the fact that the 1990s started not with the Premiership but with the Football League still intact, and with Sunderland relegated in 1990/91 it meant that Tyne–Wear hostilities would recommence in 1991/92.

Given that four out of the last five competitive derby games had been draws it didn't come as a great surprise when the first of a new decade ended in the same fashion, again 1-1.

However, what was surprising, considering the events of the subsequent decade and Newcastle's supremacy over Sunderland, particularly on Wearside, was that at this point in time Newcastle had not won competitively at Roker Park since 1956.

The home side went into the game as favourites although in truth, with just over two months of the season gone, neither side had pulled up any footballing trees so far. Sunderland were just below mid-table while Newcastle, under their Argentine manager and 1978 World Cup winner Osvaldo Ardiles, lay in a perilous position, 21st.

Nevertheless it was Newcastle who made the early running and, overall, equipped themselves well in this fixture. Although Sunderland took the lead through Peter Davenport in the 21st minute it was the visitors who scored the goal of the game with a beautiful curling 25-yard shot from Liam O'Brien at the Roker End, where the 4,000 travelling Magpie fans were housed.

By the time the return fixture came about in March 1992 Ardiles had been replaced as manager of Newcastle by their talisman, Kevin Keegan, worshipped by the Magpies and inevitably disliked by the Sunderland faithful. However, the former Hamburg player and European Footballer of the Year had a Midas touch on Tyneside that had first taken hold when he was a player at St James' Park, beginning in 1982.

His magic touch would extend into management and breathe new life into United.

Nevertheless, Keegan had a tough job on his hands just to keep the Geordies in the division, and although he would do that it was by a whisker – just four points – while Sunderland fared little better, ending just a couple of places higher than their rivals with merely one point more when the campaign finished.

One of the games that kept United up was a 1-0 victory over the Black Cats, courtesy of a David Kelly goal scored after 33 minutes. The win was deserved, especially given that early in the second half United had a clearly legitimate goal disallowed when Anton Rogan, Sunderland's no-nonsense defender, had hooked a Micky Quinn header from behind the line with Tim Carter (RIP) well beaten.

The Keegan magic took hold in 1992/93, his first full season in charge of Newcastle, when a bandwagon started to roll and rolled all the way to the Premiership. United took the lead by storm in a frenetic season that captured the imagination of the Tyneside public and led them to promotion by a country mile. In doing so they amassed 96 points, lost just once at fortress St James', and scored a more than entertaining 92 goals, conceding just 38. This was not luck, it was superb football, and while in the years to come Niall Quinn, Sunderland's soon-to-be talisman, referred to the Black Cats as being aboard a "Magic Carpet Ride", Keegan's effect was equally as inspirational, if not almost unarguably more so, as the team became known nationally, thanks to Sky television, as "the Entertainers".

It was therefore almost inevitable that the Tyne–Wear derby games of 1992/93 would produce two Newcastle wins to start a Tyneside run against their Wearside rivals that spooked Sunderland fans in the next 20 years.

United arrived at Roker Park top of the league, having not lost a game, and went away with a priceless 2-1 win courtesy of a magnificent Roker End free-kick from Liam O'Brien that sent the Magpie fans crazy. Tim Carter in the Sunderland goal never saw it until it was nestled in the back of the net. The win also left Sunderland deep in trouble with regards to league position.

The return game at St James' Park towards the end of the campaign was on a Sunday, and kicked off at midday to accommodate live television coverage, a first for the age-old fixture.

Again Newcastle triumphed, this time 1-0 courtesy of an early Scott Sellars' goal.

Losing twice to Newcastle in the same season epitomized an awful campaign for the Sunderland player-manager Terry Butcher. The Black Cats would scrape survival by the skin of their teeth despite losing dreadfully at Notts County on the last day of the season.

For Newcastle it was the start of a show that would capture the imagination of both Tyneside and English football.

Sunderland were promoted in 1995/96 under Peter Reid and would enjoy something of a renaissance themselves under the Scouser. However, a problem loomed in advance of the first Tyne–Wear encounter during the 1996/97 season when Newcastle fans were barred from a near decrepit Roker Park due to safety and security concerns. Complaints were made but the waters muddied further when an offer of 1,000 tickets to the St James' hierarchy was turned down and an inflammatory statement made by the then Magpie chief executive, Freddie Fletcher, which really wasn't needed.

Therefore, although on the face of it there were legitimate reasons why supporters were banned from each other's grounds, what we ended up with was perhaps the greatest low in the history of the Tyne–Wear rivalry.

What other local derby game in world football, at that time, could lay claim to such a dubious honour? I pondered this question at the time and couldn't come up with an equivalent. Not even the sectarian abyss of Glasgow Rangers and Glasgow Celtic had degenerated into such farce and this thus merely demonstrated, as if a demonstration were needed, the bitterness and animosity engendered by the Tyne–Wear fixture.

It is therefore doubtful whether the Sunderland v Newcastle United game on 4th September 1996 had ever been played out in such a nasty and spiteful atmosphere. A horrible, vitriolic cloud hung over Roker Park on a night where you could once more cut the atmosphere with a knife.

Newcastle won the fixture 2-1 and it was the Cockney Les Ferdinand who etched his name into Tyne–Wear derby folklore when he scored with a stunning headed winner to settle a pulsating Roker Park showdown. Ferdie's winner came 10 minutes after back-in-favour Peter Beardsley had answered manager Kevin Keegan's emergency call to fire Newcastle back into it. The £6-million striker ignited the Geordie season, breaking thousands of Wearside hearts in the process.

Alan Shearer's reaction on the final whistle typified the sheer elation of the Newcastle camp. Mass abuse from the Fulwell End fell on deaf ears as the new England captain's clenched-fist salute said it all.

However, an away victory appeared the least likely outcome at the interval as fired-up Sunderland led, courtesy of Martin Scott's 19th-minute spot kick. At that stage it was no more than Peter Reid's battlers deserved as they made a mockery of their neighbour's multi-millionaire status. With Newcastle not only confronted by such forceful opponents and a home-only crowd as hostile as any they had faced, it needed a titanic turnaround for United to avert a potential crisis.

The comeback was all the more admirable considering the storm United endured on and off the pitch earlier. For long spells in a one-sided first period it looked as if Newcastle might have crumbled, such was the abuse dished out by the Roker fans and the pressure brought to bear by wave after wave of Roker possession.

Rob Elliott was booked for a foul on Paul Stewart as Sunderland began to answer the crowd's battle cry and the Black Cats might have taken the lead on 12 minutes when skipper Kevin Ball splendidly won possession in midfield before swapping passes with Gray. Peacock half cleared but when Steve Agnew attempted to latch on to the loose ball the bounce was unkind. Agnew, however, did not have to wait too long before having a decisive impact in his first northeast derby. Again it was Ball who sprayed a pass out wide and, rather than chip towards the far post, Agnew chose to take on Elliott. It proved the correct tactic as the left-back was ruled to have tripped him just inside the box.

Martin Scott, the Sunderland full-back, proved a master of the big occasion, sending Srníček the wrong way and the fans into raptures. Then came the Ferdinand and Beardsley goals, making the mood even more hateful.

After the match Keegan summed up his reaction to the venomous atmosphere when he stated that: *"I relished it and I think the players relished it. We felt we were against the world. The only way we were going to answer our critics was out there. We knew we would have to start playing a lot better after half time. The first half was a battle. It was a typical local derby. I have never been one to say anything bad about Sunderland and Middlesbrough. I want them up here. Sunderland will turn a lot of sides over at Roker Park and there is no doubt they will stay up. They work so hard for each other."*

Sunderland skipper Kevin Ball said afterwards: *"Of course, we are disappointed. But there were a lot of good things to come out of that game. There is no need to pick ourselves up for West Ham on Sunday afternoon. We always look at the positive side of things."*

Roker scorer Martin Scott added: *"The fans were tremendous and we are upset for them. However, we played quite well, though we are not happy with the two goals that we gave away. Newcastle picked themselves up straight away in the second half and Alan Shearer and Peter Beardsley closed us down at the back and we could not get out. I thought it was a great game, though. I would have loved the game to have finished 1 v 0. Unfortunately we lost our way for 20 minutes in the second half."*

Following the match I was able to speak to some Newcastle fans from Low Fell, near Birtley, who informed me that they had managed to get tickets for the Roker End through a friend but they had left at half-time, suffering from an induced paranoia that they had been "sussed" by the Sunderland fans, such was the partisan atmosphere.

For those fans who made the match, watched by a paltry 22,037 – the last ever Tyne–Wear derby game at Roker Park – it was a night that would be indelibly etched on their minds.

On 7th January 1997, Kevin Keegan announced his resignation as manager of Newcastle United; the club released a press statement:

Newcastle United Football Club today announce the resignation of manager Kevin Keegan. Kevin informed the board of his wish to resign at the end of the season, having decided he no longer wishes to continue in football management at this stage in his life. Following lengthy discussions of which the board attempted to persuade Kevin to change his mind, both parties eventually agreed that the best route forward was for the club to, reluctantly, accept his resignation with immediate effect.

Keegan left the club with a short statement:

It was my decision and my decision alone to resign. I feel I have taken the club as far as I can, and that it would be in the best interests of all concerned if I resigned now. I wish the club and everyone concerned with it all the best for the future.

Keegan was replaced by the former Liverpool and Scotland legend Kenny Dalglish who took charge of the team for his first Tyne–Wear derby on 5th April 1997, where once again, and in a tit for tat gesture, away fans were barred from St James' Park. This time Sunderland came away with a draw, much to the delight of the few Black Cat fans who had infiltrated the stadium and to those watching the beam-back at Roker Park.

Kenny Dalglish admitted after the game that a draw was a better result for Sunderland than Newcastle. However, with Sunderland struggling in the league it was an outcome that didn't do a lot of good for either of the derby rivals. Three points would have been a tremendous boost to United's remote title hopes; instead they ended the game in fourth place.

The full three points that looked increasingly likely for the Roker men until the late intervention of Alan Shearer would have gone a long way towards assuring their survival. One point meant they had to battle on anxiously, needing two wins from their last five games – wins that ultimately didn't materialize so they were relegated once more.

"It will be a scrap from here in," agreed Roker boss Peter Reid, who was torn between delight at an unexpected away point and disappointment that it wasn't the three it could so easily have been. *"It has been a scrap for us all season. Not many people come to Newcastle and get points and if we keep going about our job in the same way, we will stay up."*

Whatever its ultimate effect, a share of the spoils was the fairest outcome from one of the better derby games. In the opening 15 minutes, it looked like a case of not who would win, but by how many, as Newcastle totally dominated. However, United lost their way, the excellent Chris Waddle began prompting Sunderland, and Lionel Perez made two brilliant blocks of one-on-one chances that Les Ferdinand and Alan Shearer should have scored from.

It wasn't as big a surprise that Waddle sent in Michael Gray to cut inside Warren Barton and Darren Peacock from the left and slot a right-footed shot past Shaka Hislop, two minutes after Robert Lee's departure. David Ginola had always looked like Newcastle's best avenue of creativity but after the Frenchman's early threat, United puzzlingly failed to use him. However, it was hardly surprising that it was Ginola who bamboozled two defenders down the left 13 minutes from time, before slinging over a cross that brought the equalizer. Barton, who after a bright start had become the fans' favourite target for their frustrations, headed down. The previously impenetrable Roker central defensive duo of Richard Ord and Lee Howey were caught flatfooted in no man's land, and Shearer pounced to volley clinically past Perez.

"Sunderland might think they were a bit unlucky, even though we perhaps had the advantage territorially," said Dalglish. *"But overall it was a fair result."*

Newcastle won through to the 1999 FA Cup final where they were ultimately defeated by Manchester United, but it was an incident before the game that would have ramifications. The Sunderland player and self-confessed Newcastle United fan Lee Clark was pictured wearing an "SMB" T-shirt (the significance of which has already been discussed) and once the picture had reached the Sunderland Stadium of Light, the new ground, his Wearside career was effectively over. Quite why he allowed himself to be put in that position was never really adequately explained.

With Sunderland relegated the two teams didn't face each other again until the last season of the 20th century, and for once it would be a campaign from which the Black Cats could claim bragging rights, at least in the northeast, as they remained undefeated against the Magpies.

The 117th league fixture between the two sides took place at an extremely wet St James' Park as the rain bucketed down. However, for the 800 Sunderland fans in attendance it probably felt like bright sunshine!

It was Kevin Phillips' predatory instincts that settled the derby on a night of red-and-white dreams and of nightmares played out in black and white. For Newcastle's shell-shocked supporters, who had endured Wembley humiliation and title near-misses, this was their most painful experience since Sunderland's last win on Tyneside nine years previous.

For the delirious visiting fans, this second Premiership victory of the season arguably eclipsed that play-off triumph. On this occasion, Sunderland came from behind after Kieron Dyer had shot United into a 28th-minute lead.

Peter Reid's side came out fighting after the break and held the upper hand long before Niall Quinn equalized in the 64th minute. As United wilted, Phillips proved the man for the big occasion, firing a superb winner to secure the Wearsiders' first league win over their neighbours for almost two decades.

But this was a night which will be remembered as much for Ruud Gullit's staggering decision to keep Alan Shearer on the bench and for the match being played in some of the most treacherous conditions both the players and the crowd will ever have experienced. The heavens had opened long before kick-off and the rain lashed down throughout, making the football almost farcical during the closing stages.

Few would have complained had referee Graham Poll abandoned proceedings with the scoreline at 1-1, but once Phillips struck in the 74th minute the referee had little option but to carry on, despite surface water turning the game into a lottery.

At half-time, Gullit must have been feeling smug as United had wrestled control from Sunderland, who had opened brightly. The Dutchman could argue that, for 45 minutes at least, his sensational decision to prefer self-confessed Mackem fan Paul Robinson to the England skipper had been vindicated. For once United took a stranglehold in midfield and, following Dyer's strike, grew in confidence.

Sunderland had kicked off in vibrant mood. After just two minutes, Phillips charged down a hesitant clearance from Alain Goma, only for on-loan keeper Tommy Wright, making his first appearance for the club since 1993, to collect. With Nick Summerbee prominent on the right flank, Sunderland stretched United. On 14 minutes, Quinn, at full stretch, only just failed to connect with a Phillips cross, while Barton was forced to concede a corner when Summerbee drove the ball into the middle.

Then Phillips attempted an audacious scissor kick from the winger's centre only to direct it into the arms of Wright. As Speed's and Dyer's influences grew, United enjoyed more of the possession, with the £6-million summer recruit breaking the deadlock with a finely worked goal.

Silvio Marić, who had started nervously, cut in from the right before feeding Robinson. The youngster fed Dyer with a delightful pass and the midfielder beat the advancing Sørensen to maintain his fine record against Sunderland.

The goal knocked the stuffing out of a previously composed Sunderland, who had Paul Butler and Phillips booked for dissent in the space of a minute. However, during this period Newcastle failed to carve out a clear-cut chance. On the stroke of half-time, the ever-alert Phillips nipped in-between Nikos Dabizas and Barton, but his ambitious volley travelled well wide.

No doubt berated by Peter Reid during the interval, Sunderland seized the initiative on the restart and looked likely scorers long before Quinn struck. Only a last-gasp challenge by the reprieved Dabizas foiled Phillips as he ran on to Quinn's flick and then the Irishman headed Summerbee's cross wide of target. Duncan Ferguson replaced Robinson on 56 minutes, though by now most of the action was heading for Wright's goal.

Summerbee's dead-ball prowess was becoming more

threatening as the conditions worsened and, from a right-wing free-kick, Quinn met the ball at the near post, glancing a deft header past Wright.

Inevitably the Shearer chants reached a crescendo, though United fans had to wait another eight minutes for his introduction. He had only been on the pitch for two minutes when Phillips demonstrated just why he was being mentioned as a genuine rival for Shearer's international shirt. Again Summerbee was the source, finding the little striker with a marvellous cross-field ball. Phillips was initially denied by the sprawling Wright but, in a flash, he spun around, retrieved possession and directed a stunning shot into the far corner of the net.

It was all too much for the disbelieving Geordies who had greeted Gullit's strange line-up with admirable restraint. Soon the name Robert Lee echoed around the stadium – a clear sign that they wouldn't tolerate his exile when there were obviously inferior players ahead of him.

Despite Sunderland handling the conditions more effectively, United still might have equalized. From Shearer's pass Nolberto Solano wasted a glorious chance in the 85th minute, shooting wide from 15 yards. But that was nothing to the escape Sunderland enjoyed in injury time. Substitute Kevin Ball, in a desperate attempt to tackle Ferguson, sent the ball looping 25 yards towards Sørensen's goal and, with the Dane stranded, it struck the bar.

The Toon Army realized it just wasn't going to be their night.

After the game it was revealed that there had been 42 arrests for criminal damage and public disorder offences. Eleven were made at the ground and 26 known troublemakers from the Sunderland area were stopped as they were making their way to St James' Park.

The final derby game of a 20th-century season was a thriller that ended all square – 2-2 – and for once it lived up to all the hype. It was a cracking game of football, although had Newcastle taken their chances in the first half hour they'd have been beyond the winning post by the interval. They ran the show for most of the first half and deservedly led 2-1, but it was Sunderland all the way in the second.

Two down inside 21 minutes to Magpie manager Bobby Robson's rampant troops, Sunderland hauled themselves back into the game to pinch a point thanks to a Kevin Phillips brace. And while Wearside fans savoured a stunning comeback, United fans could take consolation from the fact Robson had transformed their team since they last met their bitterest of rivals the previous August.

A typically tense start to this, the 118th Tyne–Wear derby, saw little of note, but the game soon exploded into life when Kevin Kilbane's run and cross from the left caused some anxious moments in the United back four. However, Newcastle hit back as Gary Speed centred from the right, and only a brilliant block by Butler sent the ball behind for Newcastle's first corner. Dyer delivered beautifully from the flag kick and Ferguson powered a header goalwards only to see Thomas Sørensen deny him with a fantastic fingertip save. Seconds later, United did what they'd threatened and silenced the Stadium of Light crowd, storming into an 11th-minute lead.

Dyer cut in from the right and slid a neat pass into Duncan Ferguson, who in turn side-footed to Didier Domi. And the Frenchman fired a left-foot shot which clipped Niall Quinn's ankles at the near post and bobbled agonizingly past the helpless Sørensen into the Sunderland net.

Sunderland almost hit back immediately as Gavin McCann lashed a free-kick through the Newcastle wall – but he was inches wide of the target. It took another top-drawer save from Sørensen, however, to keep United from forging further ahead.

Michael Gray went to sleep, allowing Dyer to race through – but the great Dane advanced bravely to block Dyer's low shot with his chest. Ferguson should have put the rebound in but scuffed his shot, and Butler blasted the ball off the line. With Sunderland all at sea, another United goal seemed almost inevitable. Makin gave away a free-kick on the left, Dyer swung the ball in and Helder rose unchallenged to head United 2-0 up with 21 minutes gone.

But gutsy Sunderland hit straight back thanks to their Little and Large strike partnership – Quinn and Kevin Phillips. Makin lofted a free-kick towards the box, Quinn flicked on and Phillips ran to gleefully slide the ball between the advancing Harper's legs and in.

With the game positively pulsating, United soon had Sunderland hearts in mouths again when Craddock cleared a Ferguson effort off the line. Before the interval though, it took a brace of brilliant saves from Easington-born keeper Steve Harper to preserve Newcastle's lead. Quinn – giving Dabizas a tricky time – nudged the ball on for Kilbane but the United keeper was equal to his deft left-foot shot. Then Makin combined cutely with Summerbee before unleashing a curler that was bound for the top corner – until Harper's fingertips intervened.

The tone was set for the second half.

As Sunderland dominated play and possession, Newcastle were content to sit tight and soak up the pressure. And despite Harper having the game of his life, the Magpies' reticence eventually cost them dearly. Sunderland laid siege to the United box as their fans turned the volume up another couple of notches. Makin – who has never scored for Sunderland – almost equalized after a brilliant pass from Summerbee. Racing into a gaping hole left by Domi, he tested Harper to the limit with a rocket shot which the United keeper tipped away tremendously. Substitute Michael Reddy fed Quinn, whose clever flick caused chaos in the Newcastle box, but the visitors somehow scrambled clear. Then Harper pulled off an equally classy save from a point-blank Kilbane strike. But seven minutes from time United cracked when Kilbane turned provider for Phillips. And Super Kev didn't miss from five yards as he turned his second chance of the afternoon into his second goal of the day.

Running to the corner of the north and east stands, he disappeared under delirious hordes of Sunderland fans, who were on the track around the pitch.

DOUBLE AGENTS?

2000/01 to 2011/12

The first few years of the 21st century would be a topsy-turvy affair in the history of both Tyne and Wear clubs as the merry-go-round of managers continued. Also, the regimes of chairmen Bob Murray at Sunderland and Freddie Shepherd at Newcastle came to an end, the former after 20 years at the helm. In the case of the Black Cats it was a former player and all-round good guy Niall Quinn who, together with the Drumaville Consortium, a group of Irish businessmen, saved the day; over on Tyneside it was an entrepreneur, Mike Ashley, a Chelsea fan, who rode in on his white horse to take on the significant challenge at Gallowgate.

The latter would be dubbed "Agent Ashley" by the Sunderland fans when United were surprisingly relegated during the decade, and although an unfair label it demonstrated once more the personal abuse that goes with the Tyne and Wear territory. The Sports Direct International PLC supremo would get on with the job at hand and by the end of the 2011/12 season he had re-engineered the fortunes of the black and whites.

Although Sunderland suffered more relegations, including some unwanted historic lows (which came as no surprise given the club's history of demotion since the mid-1980s), Newcastle United, of "the Entertainers" fame, also experienced hard times, and both clubs had to come back and rebuild from the Football League. However, with just two wins from the 16 games played between the two sides and 27 goals conceded Sunderland did not emerge from this period of just over a decade with much to shout about Tyne and Wear derby-wise. Effectively this era was about Newcastle.

Nearly 800,000 spectators would watch the derby games in the 2000/01 to 2011/12 period, a throwback to the 1950s.

Alan Shearer, the Magpies' world-record signing ace marksman retired in 2006 after scoring 206 goals for the club, a United record. However, at the beginning of the new century the lad from Wallsend Boys Club had Sunderland firmly in his sights.

Nevertheless, it wouldn't start well for Shearer and it was Sunderland who sprung the first surprise of the decade when, on 18th November 2000, they fought back magnificently against Bobby Robson's Newcastle United to record a famous and second successive victory on Tyneside. For long spells the Black Cats had to weather a Magpie storm as the home side tried to capitalize on a fourth-minute lead given to them by Gary Speed after his header had rebounded off a post.

In truth it could have been a much worse start for the visitors had Domi's through ball, after just 17 seconds, been put away by Speed, but the latter snatched his shot and scuffed it well wide. Sunderland decided not to risk the Argentine Arca who had come back from international duty and was available for selection. At half-time some supporters were ruing this.

Sunderland had their moments in the first half when Niall Quinn cleverly tried to chip Shay Given, but the United custodian was equal to the challenge and managed to scramble the ball away. At half-time it looked bad for the red and whites.

However, Sunderland came out all guns blazing in the second half and mounted an aerial assault on the home goal. This tactic paid handsome dividends just one minute after Arca had come on as a substitute, when Kevin Phillips crossed, for Hutchison to smash home.

Despite this, Newcastle rallied and the Peruvian Solano was unfortunate to see a free-kick come back off the bar with Sørensen stranded. The defining moment came with 14 minutes remaining when a left-wing Michael Gray cross was met by Quinn, who powered a magnificent picture-book header past Given to silence the huge home crowd.

There was a twist in the tale when Quinn almost turned villain after upending Robert Lee in the penalty area with just eight minutes remaining. However, while Shearer blasted the spot kick to Thomas Sørensen's left the Dane was equal to the challenge and pulled off a superb save to leave the Magpies desolate. It was the eighth time that a Newcastle player had missed a penalty kick in a Tyne–Wear derby game.

As a footnote to the game it was the Geordie boy Alan Shearer who was the captain of Newcastle United that day and, with Sunderland skippered by Wearsider Michael Gray, it was the first time in the modern era that both teams had been led by locally born players.

Although the Sunderland fans that day left St James' joyous, little did they know that in the next 12 years the Black Cats would win just one more Tyne–Wear derby match – and none on Tyneside.

In April 2001 two of the Premiership's least in-form teams battled out the 120th Tyne–Wear derby at the Stadium of Light. Sunderland went into the game with just one win out of their last 11 league games and with just seven points out of their last 33.

United had not fared much better; their victory over West Ham the previous Monday being their first in eight games. In addition United was without a clean sheet since they beat Manchester City at Maine Road on 30th September, a run of 28 games. But, on the other hand, United had only lost once in their last 12 trips to Wearside – a 1-0 victory to Sunderland in April 1980.

The atmosphere in the sell-out ground was absolutely electric before the game, although there was a minute's silence before the kick-off for Football League referee Mike North, who had collapsed and died at Southend the previous Monday.

Acuna got the game away with United attacking the North Stand End and defending the end in which their 3,500 supporters were housed.

The first half ended goalless but early in the second half the United fans held their breath when Hutchison went down after 46 minutes in the penalty area under a challenge from Dabizas. But Hutchison, who had been fouled more than any other player in the Premiership that season, made such a meal of it he was booked by referee Mike Riley.

In a niggly game Sunderland skipper Gray became the seventh player to be booked following his challenge from behind on Solano.

Just when United were beginning to get more ambitious they were struck a heavy blow when Sunderland took the lead in the 66th minute through the Frenchman Patrice Carteron. The man behind was Geordie boy Don Hutchison, who held the ball up perfectly until the French full-back had made his run: the latter duly drove a right-foot shot past Given and into the net for the opening goal – his first for Sunderland.

United came straight back and when Solano clipped in a right-wing corner Acuna got in a good looping header which Sørensen did well to fingertip over the top. United had been caught on the break for the goal and they were nearly caught again after 71 minutes, with Solano losing possession and giving Sunderland a two-against-one advantage.

With 14 minutes remaining the astute and experienced Magpie manager Bobby Robson made a triple substitution, bringing off Gallacher, Acuna and Solano and sending on Ameobi, Cordone and Griffin. The move paid off immediately when Griffin played a part in United grabbing a 76th-minute equalizer when he crossed from the right, and when Cort stabbed the ball into the middle O'Brien was there to turn it into the net for the equalizer.

It was O'Brien's first goal for United and it silenced the

Sunderland hordes.

Sunderland ended the season in the same seventh place as the previous campaign, whilst Newcastle finished four places lower but qualified for Europe again via the Intertoto (formerly Mitropa) Cup.

The FA Cup proved a disappointment to both clubs although Sunderland did make it as far as the fifth round, only to lose their first ever game on Wearside at that stage of the competition to West Ham United.

The next instalment of the series took place four months later and once more resulted in a share of the spoils. At St James' the teams played out a 1-1 draw, with Alan Shearer stamping his mark on the 121st Tyne–Wear League derby.

The former England skipper was unable to provide the dream finish to a match United could not afford to lose, but the 31-year-old did enough to suggest his recent injury-plagued days were a thing of the past. Shearer was a 75th-minute substitute as Bobby Robson's side went in search of a winning goal, and the Magpies' captain admitted:

It felt great to be out there. The crowd's reaction sent a shiver down my spine and that was just when I was warming up. The ovation when I came on was something else and all I need now is match fitness. We were pleased with our performance but there was a tinge of disappointment in the dressing room. One lapse of concentration at the back has cost us the points but we still had the chances to win the game.

Craig Bellamy won a place in the hearts of Newcastle fans everywhere when his smartly taken 43rd-minute strike cancelled out a typical piece of Kevin Phillips opportunism nine minutes earlier. Sunderland looked the better of the two teams in the first half but United, inspired by Laurent Robert, dominated proceedings after the break, and Nolberto Solano had two great, late chances to clinch the win.

In the return game of the 2001/02 season Sunderland once more failed to see off Newcastle on home soil as the visitors staged a smash-and-grab raid to clinch the points, courtesy of a 1-0 victory.

Sunderland had enjoyed a long spell of supremacy as the northeast's top dogs, having gone six derby matches unbeaten against their rivals from St James' Park, a run stretching back to 1996. A Tyne–Wear derby victory would have been an ideal tonic for Sunderland manager Peter Reid to use to lift crumbling confidence on Wearside in the closing weeks of what had been a troubled campaign at the Stadium of Light.

But Dabizas' 64th-minute header, combined with a terrific goalkeeping display from Shay Given, meant that Sunderland had to battle on as the lowest-ranked of the region's three Premiership clubs, while the Magpies flew higher and higher in the top-flight table.

Both managers had had considerable selection posers to weigh up in the build-up to the 122nd league derby meeting. But Robson's eventual line-up proved bolder than that of his Sunderland counterpart as he attempted to mastermind a memorable victory. Somewhat surprisingly, Jermaine Jenas, who had arrived at St James' Park from Nottingham Forest earlier in the month, was given his first Premiership start. The midfielder had only celebrated his 19th birthday six days earlier but Robson, who had turned 69 on the same day, clearly felt his £5-million wonder kid could cope with the pressure of the big derby occasion. He was right – Jenas never looked out of his depth.

Having spent months bringing new striker Patrick M'Boma to the Stadium of Light, Reid opted to leave him on the substitutes' bench for the first half, with Niall Quinn soldiering on alongside Kevin Phillips. Joachim Björklund made his home debut but Julio Arca, the undisputed star of the previous season's Stadium of Light showdown, missed out due to a groin problem.

The Black Cats started off well: Andy O'Brien had to be alert to deny Claudio Reyna an early opener, while Kevin Phillips missed a golden chance to register his fifth Sunderland goal against the Magpies shortly afterwards. Craig Bellamy, who had scored on his derby debut at St James' Park the previous August, beat Thomas Sørensen again on 16 minutes, only to be denied by an offside flag. The pacy Welshman burst through again five minutes later, this time lobbing his shot over both keeper and bar.

Scoring goals from midfield had been a problem for the Wearsiders during the season and Kevin Kilbane showed why after 25 minutes, when he lifted the ball over the crossbar from close range.

Beating the old enemy at home was a problem for the Black Cats and not since 1980 had red and white conquered black and white in their own backyard.

Reid introduced M'Boma for Quinn at the start of the second half, giving the Cameroon international his first taste of competitive action since facing Egypt in Mali on 4th February. This should have given the Black Cats fresh attacking impetus, however, just after the hour mark Nikos Dabizas, Newcastle's giant Greek defender, made his mark instead, after M'Boma had been shown a yellow card for a foul on Aaron Hughes. Laurent Robert delivered a precise free-kick from the left, Alan Shearer flicked the ball on and Dabizas pounced at the back post to head it firmly past Sørensen and spark celebrations among the visiting supporters.

Sunderland had a torrid time during the campaign and escaped relegation by the skin of their teeth, whilst Newcastle enjoyed themselves and ended up in a Champions League spot. The FA Cup also provided other high notes for the Geordies as they reached the sixth round, although it was Middlesbrough who stole the show northeast-wise, as they reached the semi-finals.

The 2002/03 season would be a disaster for Sunderland. They imploded, accumulated just 19 Premier League points, the lowest ever, and for the first time in their long history finished bottom of a league. To pile the agony on to the Black Cats Newcastle United did the double over them and finished third in the league to once more qualify for the Champions League. There would be no more meetings between the two sides for nearly two and a half years.

The first of Newcastle's two wins came at St James' in the September and was watched by over 52,000 spectators. It was Newcastle's first home Premiership victory over Sunderland, as in their previous four visits to St James' Park the Black Cats had won twice and picked up two draws. However, on this occasion United got their revenge with a 2-0 victory.

Alan Shearer led United out still wearing a bandage on his head – legacy of the three stitches he had had inserted in the previous Wednesday night's Champions League defeat in Kiev – but despite the fact that both teams had struggled lately the atmosphere in St James' Park was nothing short of incredible.

United lined up with Andy Griffin at right-back and Aaron Hughes on the left, but Sunderland went into the game in a defensive mood and were caught out after 85 seconds when Craig Bellamy gave United the lead and, in doing so, grabbed his first goal of the season.

Shearer doubled United's lead in the 39th minute when he was bundled down by McAteer right on the edge of the penalty area. The referee Mike Riley immediately blew for a United free-kick which Solano took, rolling the ball sideways for Shearer to drive a low right-foot shot past the defensive wall and inside Sørensen's right-hand post.

Seven months later it was a 43rd-minute penalty that sunk Sunderland at the Stadium of Light. When Newcastle United were awarded the spot kick following Kevin Kilbane's foul on Craig

Bellamy it was not immediately clear who was going to take it as the regular taker, Alan Shearer, was sitting injured in the visiting dugout.

However, it was the Peruvian Nobby Solano who grabbed the ball, although the fact that his last penalty was a miss against Middlesbrough at St James' Park two seasons previously may well have been uppermost in the minds of the visiting Toon Army. Despite this, he made no mistake, sending the Sunderland custodian, Thomas Sørensen, the wrong way, and slipping in the match-winning goal. In fact, Solano succeeded where Shearer had not in scoring a penalty past the Danish international to grab his 37th goal for United.

Bobby Robson warned his players before the game that despite Sunderland's lowly league position they would fight every inch of the way and they duly did.

The second half was played in the same vein as the first, with United creating a lot of reasonable chances; however, a second goal would just not come for them, adding to the tension as the Black Cats went in search of an equalizer. To alleviate this, Jonathan Woodgate, at the heart of the United defence, played an exceptional game.

Newcastle left the Stadium of Light not knowing when they would return but, more importantly, they left with three crucial points, which all but ensured that Champions League football would be played on Tyneside the next season. For Sunderland it was another nail in their relegation coffin.

Sunderland spent two seasons in the wilderness of the Football League but were promoted in 2004/05 at a canter, winning the division by seven points. However, the resumption of hostilities with their old rivals ended in a familiar way: defeat, twice, enabling United to record successive league doubles over the Black Cats.

In advance of the 125th Tyne–Wear derby at St James' Park on 23rd October 2005 Sunderland's Tommy Miller revealed that

Sunderland were ready to land a knockout blow on Newcastle as they had been having secret boxing lessons! Boss Mick McCarthy had introduced a killer new training session into Sunderland's regime, with players pulling on boxing gloves and beating up punchbags.

Miller reckoned that Sunderland were ready to knuckle down and dish out a blow to Graeme Souness, Newcastle's manager, that was to prove fatal. He said: *"We have been boxing. It is quite a session, punch bags and weights, lots of aggression. It toughens us up and gets you ready for the battle!"*

It was a novel way of limbering up for such a tense encounter but in the end it was to no avail as Newcastle, on home soil, won an absorbing match 3-2 and Graeme Souness celebrated his first Tyne–Wear derby with a victory. This was in sharp contrast to previous games against Portsmouth and Wigan Athletic when United couldn't string two passes together.

With Sunderland determined to put on a good show, the capacity crowd and the millions watching on television were treated to a real feast of football. But the most important thing for Newcastle was that all three points found their way into their larder as they scored more than one Premiership goal at St James' Park for the first time since 27th February.

The talk before the match was that Souness faced the chop should those three points not come United's way. The other talking point through the week in the northeast was the likely absence of Michael Owen and the fact that the England international was going to watch the game from the stands. Shola Ameobi was his replacement and the manager was amply rewarded for that faith in selecting him, as the forward claimed two goals, even though the second appeared to go in off Steve Caldwell. And when the former United defender brought down the gangling striker, Emre stepped up to hit a superb winning goal direct from the free-kick.

Unfortunately, on a day when United suddenly found their

shooting boots, the defence, which had only leaked one goal in their previous three games, suddenly let in the water. And the reason was that their £8.5-million man, Jean-Alain Boumsong, played poorly and looked like a player whose confidence was rock-bottom.

Sunderland scored their two goals through Lawrence and Elliott in the space of six minutes just before the interval, and the general feeling at half-time was that if Sunderland had grabbed the next goal then they might have gone on to win the fixture after three defeats on the bounce against United. Sunderland put a lot into the game and their work rate was outstanding.

The general verdict though was that it had been a belter of a derby match, with United just having that extra bit of class to ensure the three points went their way.

If Sunderland had put up a good show at St James' Park they did anything but in the return on Wearside as they slumped to a humiliating 1-4 home defeat to end the game bottom of the Premier League, with 12 points.

As the match finished it was clear there were few home fans that had stayed on; United succeeded in clearing the stadium with their best victory at Sunderland since Boxing Day 1955 and their 50th success over their nearest rivals.

However, in the first hour United were nothing short of pathetic, and Sunderland's first home league win of the season looked very much on the cards. In that first half the home side had been superior in midfield, with the United pairing in the centre – of Lee Clark and Amdy Faye – not gelling, and contributing to a really terrible performance from the visitors.

However, the Magpies manager, Glenn Roeder, made inspired substitutions, particularly Michael Chopra for Clark, with Kieron Dyer dropping back into midfield, a move that had an immediate effect.

Chopra's 60th-minute equalizer with his first touch of the ball changed the whole course of the game as Sunderland suddenly looked as if they should be where they were – rock-bottom. It started to rain goals for United, with Alan Shearer wiping out his penalty miss of a few years back against Sunderland at St James' Park after young Charles N'Zogbia had been fouled.

Charlie's goal five minutes later when he beat Hoyte, Miller and Collins in a mazy run before slotting the ball home was superb but it got better when Shearer's substitute Albert Luque ran through the middle to grab his first goal for the club.

So United won the game with that three-goal burst in six minutes midway through the second half, which meant that they had picked up 10 points out of 12 in the four derby matches with Sunderland and Middlesbrough.

Chopra's equalizer changed the whole game and was the fastest goal ever by a substitute in the history of the Tyne–Wear encounter. No wonder the 22-year-old striker said after the game: *"I've had to wait a long time for my first Premiership goal – but for it to come against Sunderland makes it worthwhile. Every time I've been on the pitch this season, I've tried to give it my best shot and to score against Sunderland with my first touch was a dream come true. When you grow up in Newcastle, you dream about playing against Sunderland and it's been a pleasure to be involved in two of them."*

For Alan Shearer it was a bittersweet game. Stretchered from the field of play injured, it would be his last game in a black-and-white shirt.

Sunderland were subsequently relegated with a mere 15 points whilst Newcastle not only qualified for the Intertoto Cup but could also look back in satisfaction on an FA Cup campaign that saw them reach the sixth round before eventually succumbing to Chelsea at Stamford Bridge.

The two teams would not meet again until the 2007/08 season.

By that time the former Sunderland player Sam Allardyce was the United manager, although his tenure was coming under increasing scrutiny due to the manner of the football that the black and whites played. A 1-1 draw in October 2007 was therefore acceptable but, in truth, Sunderland kicked themselves for not taking all three points from the match.

Indeed, had James Milner's cross not ended up in the Sunderland net in the 65th minute to give the visitors a fortuitous equalizer, United would probably have lost and the roof would have caved in for them and their manager since before the match Sunderland's tally of five goals at home was the lowest of any of the other teams in the Premier League.

Sunderland scored after 52 minutes due to shambolic defending from the Magpies. The move that led to the goal started when Abdoulaye Faye was panicked into a mistake by the impressive Kenwyne Jones, and David Rozehnal had to concede a left-wing corner. When Jones took the short corner he could have played it to either Grant Leadbitter or Carlos Edwards without a United player in sight. The powerful striker chose the former, and when the cross came into the middle, Rozehnal and Charles N'Zogbia left Danny Higginbotham unmarked to head Sunderland ahead.

This typified the visitors' performance as the United marking was non-existent all afternoon. Sunderland's opener meant United really had problems, for every time they had gone behind that season they had lost and it was hard to see how this sequence was going to come to an end before Milner's fluke equalizer.

However, an equalizer did come and when it did it knocked the stuffing out of Sunderland, so much so that for a while it looked as though United were going to pull off a win they would not have deserved. And while Michael Chopra went the closest to doing this with a header that hit the United crossbar, Michael Owen – captain for the day – made a late chance for himself following a long kick from Steve Harper. But the effort needed to take him past two defenders took too much out of Owen, and his weak left-foot shot went tamely into Craig Gordon's arms.

Roy Keane, the Sunderland manager, summed it up succinctly: *"I think Sam will be happier than me tonight."*

The return game, five months later, had an all-too familiar ring about it: a Newcastle win, this time 2-0, although the Magpies did not play that well.

Roy Keane had all week to devise his tactics and plans for his first visit to St James' as a manager but they didn't work out. His ploy of playing Kenwyne Jones up front on his own never looked like working, and when Keane sent on Michael Chopra to support the former Southampton man it was far too late. Sunderland only had one chance all game, a Jones header in the 68th minute, and this brought a magnificent save out of Steve Harper, the home custodian.

Up front for Newcastle, Obafemi Martins was unusually subdued while Mark Viduka ran himself into the ground. Viduka's big contribution was the part he played in Michael Owen's penalty on the stroke of half-time with some typical nifty feet, and while the former Liverpool player's spot kick wasn't the best he will ever take, the end product was all that mattered.

However, it was the crucial first goal that knocked the stuffing out of Sunderland in the fourth minute. Geremi's cross was a good one and Owen's header was absolutely perfect, leaving the former Hearts keeper, Craig Gordon, grasping fresh air.

Owen's match-winning brace put him on to the dozen mark for the season, and the only disappointment of the day was that he did not go on and complete his hat-trick. But the result was the main thing and it meant that United had now won the six of the last seven derby matches with Sunderland.

The days of Niall Quinn and Kevin Phillips seem like a million years ago; however, some Tyne–Wear derby good news was just around the corner for the Black Cats. On 25th October 2008

Sunderland at last beat their reviled rivals at home for the first time since 1980. Regrettably though, Sunderland were reprimanded by the Football Association for failing to control their supporters due to three small but separate pitch invasions.

Sunderland were billed as favourites in the pre-match build-up and they played like favourites on the day itself, taking the game to the Magpies from first whistle to last. With the exception of a 15-minute spell before half-time, Sunderland were always the more threatening of the two sides and could, in the closing stages, have made it an even more comprehensive victory.

Sunderland manager Roy Keane's decision to start Dwight Yorke was an astute one: the veteran Trinidad and Tobago international sat in front of the back four as a protective shield with an eye for a killer pass. Dean Whitehead was also superb, relishing the physical tussle in the centre of midfield and allowing Richardson and Steed Malbranque to concentrate on trying to hurt the opposition going forward.

It worked beautifully in the 20th minute when Yorke executed a perfect Cruyff turn on the halfway line to wrong-foot Newcastle's midfield. He fed Pascal Chimbonda who moved the ball on to Malbranque. The former Spurs man took advantage of the space in front of him to cut inside, and although his cross to the unmarked Cissé was probably an attempted shot, his fellow Frenchman stabbed the ball home.

Having got in front, Sunderland handed the initiative to Newcastle, Ameobi decided to shoot rather than square to the unmarked Duff, before both Geremi and Martins had efforts charged down by some frantic Sunderland defending. Ameobi, though, was proving to be a problem and when the former England Under-21 international drew a foul from Chimbonda on the edge of the area, Anton Ferdinand lost him in the resulting free-kick and Ameobi headed Newcastle level at the far post.

If anything, Newcastle looked the stronger of the two sides as half-time approached, and they should have gone in front on the hour mark when Ameobi, fed by Martins, shifted the ball on to his weaker left foot and shanked a shot from the edge of the area wide. It proved to be pivotal as Sunderland, lifted by the introduction of Kenwyne Jones as a substitute for Yorke, went close through Cissé, only for Shay Given to save at his feet after Coloccini had got enough on the ball to direct it closer to the goalkeeper.

Malbranque also went close with a volley but Sunderland's winner eventually came.

El-Hadji Diouf was cynically tripped on the edge of the area by Butt as he went to collect a one-two from Jones, so Richardson stepped up to lash a free-kick past Given. It was a great goal to win on a great occasion for Sunderland AFC.

Sunderland kept their unbeaten run against Newcastle going in the return fixture, although they could not produce another famous win as a tight affair ended 1-1 to leave the Magpies just two points from the foot of the Premier League.

Losing to Sunderland twice in a season for the first time since 1967 would have been a low point for United but, thanks to an improved second-half performance, and a rare bit of fortune for Joe Kinnear's side, there was no double for the visitors.

There was an attempt to stir the home fans into chorus before the game when Graham Danby belted out a rousing rendition of the *Blaydon Races* but even the backing of the famed Toon Army was never going to be enough to deliver the three points, and Sunderland left St James' Park thinking that they should really have celebrated their first double for 42 years.

However, by the time Sunderland had opened the scoring with a 33rd-minute goal from Cissé, Newcastle could have been ahead themselves. José Enrique's centre looked to have unlocked the door for Andy Carroll, who considered himself unlucky to clip the top of the bar, while a great first-half chance for Ameobi – when he almost picked out the Sunderland fans on Level 7 with a howler of an effort – could have helped change the course of the game.

However, a goal-line clearance from debutant Kevin Nolan in the first half proved to be a telling contribution after Kenwyne Jones had stabbed goalwards following Kieran Richardson's free-kick, which hit the base of the post. Newcastle had cancelled out Djibril Cissé's opener thanks to Shola Ameobi's 50th goal of his Toon career after 67 minutes. In the end, Newcastle fans were grateful for Chopra's inability to be consistent in front of goal and delighted to see Andy Reid's fizzing effort at the death flash past the other side of the post.

Sunderland fans were the happier of the two sets of supporters by the end as they maintained the bragging rights after taking four points from the six on offer this season. However, when they arrived back at Central railway station for the journey home to Wearside there was crowd disorder that resulted in 32 arrests for various misdemeanours, with Newcastle fans hurling bottles, cans and glasses at the 700 red and whites.

Although disaster was avoided for Newcastle on derby day end-of-season relegation was not far off as the Magpies dropped into the relegation place following a last-day defeat at Aston Villa. While Sunderland survived to fight another Premier League campaign, there would be no more Tyne–Wear derby games for two seasons as the men from Gallowgate grappled with life in the Football League.

However, if Newcastle were looking to exact humiliation on their near neighbours to eliminate the memory of the Championship then they couldn't have done much more than thrash Sunderland 5-1 at St James' Park when they next met.

Their captain, Kevin Nolan, plundered a derby hat-trick to hand manager Chris Hughton the perfect ending to an eventful week as Newcastle routed Sunderland. The midfielder put the home side 2-0 ahead within 34 minutes and completed his treble 15 minutes from time, after striker Shola Ameobi had helped himself to two goals, the first of them from the penalty spot. It was the first hat-trick in the fixture since Peter Beardsley achieved the feat for Newcastle in January 1985.

Sunderland, who had former Magpies defender Titus Bramble sent off for an ill-judged challenge on Andy Carroll in the 53rd minute, were never at the races on a day when their promoted neighbours won at St James' Park for the first time in five attempts. Darren Bent's last-minute strike was no consolation for the travelling fans, many of whom had already left, and it proved a sweet afternoon for Hughton, following a week during which speculation over his future at the club had reached fever pitch. The 51-year-old was serenaded by the delighted home contingent in a crowd of 51,988 as his side completely outplayed their most bitter rivals, who rarely troubled goalkeeper Tim Krul until Bent's late effort, despite Geordie manager Steve Bruce sending on record signing Asamoah Gyan before half-time to add firepower.

Sunderland had conceded only seven goals in their first nine Barclays Premier League games, but were repeatedly torn apart by a committed Magpies side even before Bramble's premature departure.

The Black Cats arrived on Tyneside in an optimistic mood on the back of a seven-game unbeaten Barclays Premier League run, to meet a side which had not won on their own pitch in four attempts. But Sunderland's goals-against total was to rise significantly inside a rousing opening 45 minutes during which Newcastle took the game by the scruff of the neck.

The Magpies were on the front foot from the off as the game started at a lively pace, and they steadily built momentum before exploding into life with 24 minutes gone. It took a fine reaction save from Simon Mignolet to keep out Andy Carroll's bullet header, and the Belgian had to be equally alert two minutes later to claw

Joey Barton's stinging drive away from the bottom corner. But the deadlock was finally broken from the resulting corner when central defender Mike Williamson got up well to head down Barton's corner and Nolan sent the ball into the roof of the net with an acrobatic overhead kick. The noise level at St James' Park reached ear-splitting levels as Nolan was mobbed by his team-mates, and it was to get much, much better for the home fans before the half-time whistle sounded.

Newcastle increased their lead within eight minutes when Carroll's scuffed volley fell perfectly for the criminally unmarked Nolan, who controlled before slipping the ball past the advancing Mignolet.

Bruce's game plan was simply not working, with lone striker Bent almost redundant, and the manager made his tactical move five minutes before the break when he sent on £13-million-plus man Gyan in place of Ahmed Elmohamady and switched to a 4-4-2 formation. But before the new arrival could make an impact, his side fell further behind, after Nedum Onuoha's clumsy injury-time challenge on Jonás Gutiérrez prompted referee Phil Dowd to point to the spot. Ameobi, who had converted a penalty in the corresponding fixture two seasons ago, repeated the feat to pile the pressure on Bruce and his players.

Sunderland's reshuffle had seen Steed Malbranque drop into a midfield four and Jordan Henderson move out to the right, and while that gave them a better shape, they caused few problems for their hosts in the opening minutes of the second half. Their woes deepened with 53 minutes gone when, in his eagerness to prevent Carroll from racing in on goal, Bramble launched himself into a desperate challenge which sent the striker sprawling, and was punished with a straight red card.

Carroll sent a towering header over the bar two minutes later with the visitors rocking, and, with things going from bad to worse, Bruce introduced Kieran Richardson as a replacement for Danny Welbeck.

Krul, who had been a virtual spectator for much of the game, had to get down well to turn away Phil Bardsley's 65th-minute strike, but the Magpies were coasting to victory. They increased their lead with 20 minutes remaining when Carroll's powerful header came back off the crossbar and Ameobi rifled home spectacularly.

There was worse to come five minutes later when Nolan met Ameobi's flick-on two yards out to complete his hat-trick, and Bent's last-minute strike repaired none of the damage inflicted on the demoralized visitors.

The 132nd league derby game produced the series' fifth 1-1 draw since 2000/01 and the looks on the players' faces at full-time confirmed one of football's great truisms: better to be a lucky player than a good one. Newcastle United bossed the game, but Sunderland were celebrating at the final whistle and whilst the Football Association investigated the events following Asamoah Gyan's equalizer, the Magpies were asking how it happened.

Sunderland had trailed for 42 minutes with few hints of an equalizer until Steve Harper pushed Phil Bardsley's driven cross shot into Gyan's path. *"It summed up his day,"* joked manager Steve Bruce afterwards. *"It hit his chest and bounced five yards!"* It also epitomized a low-quality game. It quickly descended into a thud-and-blunder affair, with meaty tackles aplenty and passing moves almost non-existent. The referee Howard Webb kept control on the field, but off it things got out of hand once the ball nestled in Newcastle's net. A supporter ran on and appeared to push Harper, and when the players should have been swapping shirts, rival fans were angrily exchanging seats.

It had been first blood to Newcastle, Ahmed Elmohamady leaving the field for four minutes to have his lip stitched. By the time he returned, Sunderland ought to have been trailing although Joey Barton's exquisite pass perhaps gave Ameobi too much time to think about how he would score his seventh derby goal. Three minutes into his first match back from injury, the striker coolly ignored the onrushing Craig Gordon to guide the ball with his left foot, but put it the wrong side of the post. It was the last time he put a foot wrong.

While he looked sharp, Darren Bent, Sunderland's ace marksman, was again rusty. Unconvincing ever since he found the St James' Park net the previous October, he volleyed at Harper when Steed Malbranque launched a counter-attack. A lunging tackle on Bardsley prompted an ugly exchange in the opening quarter of an hour and Bardsley seemed to try to retaliate with a stamp but thankfully it did not connect. It would not be long, however, before Smith's afternoon was cut short, when he fell victim to Richardson's raking tackle. His parting gesture to the fans who baited him as he limped off was not very clever and the post-match sight of his ankle in a cast was not too encouraging for the Magpies.

Sunderland's only sustained pressure came midway through the first half, Malbranque forcing a good low save from Harper, and Elmohamady volleying into a crowd of players when the goalkeeper spilled the resulting corner to him. Bent's shot was blocked when Jordan Henderson rolled a short free-kick to him.

As the first half reached its conclusion, Newcastle reasserted control. Ameobi won everything in the air and Sunderland's stand-in captain, Titus Bramble, looked nothing like the super-cool defender who had dominated every other team this season.

A scorer in his last three derbies, Ameobi perhaps should have made it four when he rose above his friend at a corner, but could not keep his header down. He got closer than Barton did from a free-kick not a million miles from where Richardson scored Sunderland's winner in 2008.

The pair made amends in the 52nd minute, Ameobi heading down Barton's corner, Nolan back heeling into the net. Leon Best immediately almost doubled the lead, but could not reach José

Enrique's delivery. When he did, it hit the side-netting. Jonás Gutiérrez shot wide after cutting on to his right, and when Ameobi went past Anton Ferdinand as if he was not there, there was no one to pick out when he reached the byeline.

There was little inspiration for Steve Bruce to summon from the bench and it showed, 20 minutes of huff and puff producing little to panic the visitors. Harper's misjudgement, pushing the ball into danger, saved face for Sunderland, but the true story of this derby was not to be found on the scoreboard.

By the time the next campaign came around Newcastle United were a club transformed player-wise. However, whilst the faces changed the club's spirit since relegation remained as strong as ever as yet another derby win showed, this time 1-0. It had been a summer to forget for the Magpies, but, when Sunderland are the opposition, memories of a wonderful 21st century to date against their bitter rivals spurred them on. Led by Argentinian captain Fabricio Coloccini, the visitors summoned up the esprit de corps to triumph in an unseasonably early derby.

The pre-match body language would be replicated at the final whistle. Fifteen minutes before kick-off, coaches John Carver and Steve Stone ended the warm-up by taking Newcastle's players over to the away end. This got a few early boos out of the crowd of nearly 45,000 home fans. At the final whistle they were back, not quite as orderly but wearing more gleeful expressions.

While Alan Pardew grinned from ear to ear on the bench, lapping up the hostile atmosphere moments before kick-off, Steve Bruce stood grim-faced in Sunderland's technical area. Every time the Wallsend-raised manager takes a step forward in the Black Cats' fans' affection, along comes a derby to push him back into his place. His team's early football, however, put a smile on those craggy features, especially Stéphane Sessègnon revelling in the space he found when dropping off Asamoah Gyan.

It took just 13 seconds for the Benin international to have a shot and although it did not trouble Tim Krul, two later in the half would. Gyan nearly opened the scoring with the half's last touch, a curling left-footer a fraction from Krul's top corner, which came from an Ahmed Elmohamady knock-down. With Simon Mignolet lumping the ball forward, Sunderland's first half was one of wasted opportunities: Elmohamady headed embarrassingly wide at a near-post corner, Sessègnon hit fresh air instead of one of the Egyptian's crosses, Jack Colback failed to make decent contact on a delivery, Gyan was unable to contort his body enough to successfully redirect a Sebastian Larsson corner, and Elmohamady dummied a cross after excellent work by the tigerish Lee Cattermole.

Sunderland then got lucky when the officials somehow failed to spot Larsson tipping Barton's header around the post with his hand. A Cattermole foul on Jonás Gutiérrez allowed Ryan Taylor to hit his free-kick into the far top corner of the net as Mignolet flapped beneath it. With namesake Steven desperately trying to steal the goal, it could have been any old Taylor on the scoresheet. That goal came in the 62nd minute, by which time Newcastle had a big foothold in the game.

Sunderland were by some distance first out of the dressing room for the second half, but only in the physical sense. Pardew won the tactical battle hands down, smothering the threat of Sessègnon. Bruce's response was simply to throw on more strikers – finishing with four – while taking off Larsson, the man most capable of finding the heads of Ji and Connor Wickham.

Phil Bardsley was sent off at the end, one meaty tackle too many on a day of plenty.

Another defeat by Newcastle and a continuation of Sunderland's poor form from the previous campaign meant that on 30th November 2011 Steve Bruce was sacked as manager of Sunderland AFC. In the days following his departure a quite unique perspective from, amongst others, Sir Alex Ferguson, Bruce's former boss at Manchester United, was given on the news.

When asked to comment, Ferguson clearly stated that Bruce's Geordie roots had not helped matters at the Stadium of Light and that, ultimately, a failure to defeat Newcastle United in the northeast derby matches had sealed the former centre-half's fate.

Some Sunderland fans had never accepted him and the 1-5 defeat at the hands of Newcastle United at St James' Park during the 2010/11 season was the straw that broke the camel's back for them.

Others saw the Geordie connection as an "excuse" that would subsequently be mentioned by Bruce in media interviews to justify some very poor results. Given the fact that Bob Stokoe, who played for Newcastle United for years, was widely revered as "the Messiah" on Wearside and, indeed, had a statue erected to him outside the Stadium of Light South Stand, and that many of the Sunderland supporters are Geordies themselves, Bruce's assertion doesn't really bear close inspection.

It's a nice sound bite but nothing more than that.

Nevertheless, Bruce had once stated: *"I have always been a Newcastle lad, and when I was a lad I crawled under the turnstiles to get in, trying to save a bob or whatever it was. They were my team, I went to support them as a boy and being a Geordie it's inbred, you follow the club and it's still the same today."*

That statement was remembered by a minority of Sunderland fans. For the majority his roots didn't matter.

Revelling in the Sunderland fans' angst, many Newcastle fans mockingly referred to the Wearside club's former boss as "Agent Bruce"; the inference was clear – Sunderland's poor form was an inside job by one of their own.

It was ironic given Bruce's allegiance that when the next Black Cat manager was announced on 3rd December 2011 it was Martin

O'Neill, a Sunderland fan since the days of Charlie Hurley, who was given the hot seat.

In advance of the return game at St James on 4th March 2012 both teams warmed up for the Tyne–Wear derby game with poor results. In Sunderland's case it was a rare thrashing for a rejuvenated Black Cat side, 0-4 at the Hawthorns, whilst for the Magpies they had let slip a two-goal advantage at home to Wolves, to eventually share the points following a 2-2 draw.

Sunderland went into the match with a pathetic derby record of just two wins in 15 attempts; they hadn't won on Tyneside in 12 years. Martin O'Neill had no illusions about the task ahead:

It's as big as it gets in this country and we have to be strong and really compete. We will do our best; in fact, we need to do better than our best. It's a very, very big game and one of those games you want to do well in. I couldn't possibly treat this game lightly, nor would I ever be allowed to.

Cheick Tioté, Newcastle's Ivory Coast international, went further:

If we have to die on the pitch to win, we have to die on the pitch, if that is what we have to do to win the game. The fans have reminded me what this game means, but the history? Well I know about it, it is something I have learned since being here. When I arrived I did not know any of it, but now I will never ever forget it. I can say that is the same for every player. Newcastle against Sunderland is the biggest game for this club; it does not get any bigger.

The game was explosive. The first booking, typically, came after just 40 seconds when Lee Cattermole clattered into Tioté. For the rest of the half Newcastle allowed themselves to be sucked into a war of attrition and paid the price when, after 24 minutes, Williamson held back Sunderland's Turner and the referee had no option but to give a penalty which the Black Cats' Danish international, Nicklas Bendtner, calmly slotted home past Krul.

After 19 minutes an almighty scuffle broke out down by the Gallowgate involving the majority of the players, an unseemly incident that would subsequently earn Sunderland a £20,000 fine by the FA, and double that amount for Newcastle due to a previous misdemeanour.

It emerged after the game that at half-time the Newcastle goalkeeping coach Andy Woodman had been dismissed after a spat with Sunderland fitness coach Jim Henry as they went down the tunnel. The news came as no surprise due to the tension and emotion that had been generated in the first 45 minutes.

The second half started with Newcastle on top, something that would be maintained throughout the period. The introduction of Ben Arfa into the home side's attack caused problems for Sunderland, as he probed and crossed, giving Richardson, the visiting full-back, a difficult time. The latter would be substituted and replaced by Wayne Bridge as a result.

Sessègnon, a class act who had arguably been Sunderland's best player on the day, had been sent off after an hour's play as a result of an errant elbow. In doing so the Benin international became the sixth Sunderland player to be sent off in the history of Tyne–Wear derby matches; Newcastle has never had a man sent off in the series of games.

This left the visitors with the task of holding out for the last 30 minutes with 10 men: a tall order. Just when it looked as though it wouldn't be Newcastle's day Fraizer Campbell, Sunderland's new England international, slid in, felled Ameobi – who had himself come on as a substitute – inside the box, and the home side had the lifeline of a penalty. Ba, normally impressive for United, watched in horror as Mignolet, the Black Cats' Belgian international custodian, saved brilliantly low to his left-hand side, although clearly a yard off his line as the kick was taken.

As the clock ticked down to a home defeat Ameobi popped up to knock the ball past Mignolet in the 91st minute to earn Newcastle a well-deserved draw, although there was a suspicion of offside about it. It was Shola's seventh goal in 12 Tyne–Wear derby match appearances. Remarkably, this was the 24th consecutive time that Newcastle had scored in a Tyne–Wear derby game, stretching all the way back to 1991. Easily a series record.

As if that wasn't enough, Cattermole continued his arguments off the field after the final whistle had blown and was duly sent off for his troubles. Eight bookings, a scored penalty, a missed penalty, an injury-time disputed goal, a half-time skirmish in the tunnel, two men sent off, a crowd of 52,388 and honours even.

One wondered what the two billionaire owners, Ellis Short (Sunderland) and Mike Ashley (Newcastle United), neither of whom are natives of the area, made of it all. Short, the unassuming but decisive Dallas-born hedge-fund specialist, perhaps longed for his Skibo Castle retreat, where he could reflect in peace on the frenetic events of the day.

The arguments, however, raged in the pubs and clubs around the northeast well into the night and the sore heads that would emerge the next morning could contemplate that this had been the norm since the 19th century when games between Tyneside and Wearside's finest football clubs had begun. Although battle would recommence at a later date a sporting rivalry wrapped up in nearly 400 years of social history had, for now, come to an end.

THE FINAL WHISTLE

In May 2005, the "Passionate people. Passionate places" regional image campaign was launched to promote northeast England as a great place in which to work, study, visit and invest. A former UK industrial powerhouse had to reinvent itself as the old industries died and new ones provided the potential for people of the region to once more demonstrate their traditional skills of being quick learners, entrepreneurs and hard workers. Perhaps, though, the most powerful characteristic of the region is the good humour and welcome that awaits the visitor.

Whilst social deprivation levels remain a talking point, the optimism of the people is not in question. The region has many things going for it. Passion for life is one of its biggest assets, a love of sport is another as demonstrated by Durham Cricket Club's constant fight and eventual success in becoming England's newest (and we think best) professional county club. However, football is our biggest sport. Put passion and football together and you have a potent force. The Newcastle United – Sunderland AFC rivalry may be bitter but it has endured and it has no place for the faint-hearted.

Put simply, for as long as the game of Association Football is played teams representing the cities of Newcastle and Sunderland will battle for supremacy. At stake are not only points, a cup run or pride but a place in local folklore. It's arguable (it's always arguable in the northeast) if there is anything quite like football in the hearts and minds of the Geordies or the Mackems, and the wildly optimistic assertion that their teams are "the greatest that the world has ever seen", whilst open to question (but break it gently!) in the wider world, is fact to those of a red-and-white or black-and-white persuasion.

Although it was ever thus with football fans it almost defies explanation that both clubs can attract the volume of support that they do given the paucity of success, as measured by trophies won. In truth neither has won much in decades but to the believer their day will come. When it does, boy, will football witness something special!

The region is fortunate to have two such wonderful football clubs and it is extremely sad that the fixtures boil over into vitriol that has often resulted in violence on a massive scale and horrendous criminality. Maybe one day everyone will see sense but in the meantime it's a salient reminder of the encounter's violent social roots and the difficulty that the authorities have in policing such fixtures. In such an open-hearted region the polarization of views when it comes to football is a direct contradiction. Perhaps it's worth a study in itself, although this book may provide some evidence of why this contradiction exists.

As a result of increasing violence, the number of fixtures that the two clubs are able to play against each other has been reduced. In the 19th century as many as 35 games in a decade were viable, now you're lucky if it's half that, as "friendly" matches are simply not possible. Relegation, particularly for Sunderland, has also historically produced fewer Tyne–Wear encounters to such a degree that by the 1990s the two first teams met only eight times.

If the founders of both clubs could be brought back to life for one day I wonder what they would make of their creations? If you asked them the question of how they envisaged both clubs turning out what would they say? Who knows, but their history is everything to both clubs.

The ultimate irony is that whilst at least for one day the supporters of the rival clubs may "hate" each other, without each other what would there be to look forward to? Do Newcastle fans really wish for a world that did not include Sunderland? Would Sunderland fans really wish for season upon season of derby-less days? It's a question worth pondering and, for the more rational amongst the two clubs' followers, the answer must quite simply be that this game is ultimately their raison d'être. To do without it is to render both clubs meaningless. Why would there be a wish to end such a magnificent rivalry? Even when the clubs are in different divisions there is always the anticipation that derby day will once more come around – and the feeling that you had better be ready for it.

So which club is the best? The opening pages of this book state that victory for one side over the other indicates a temporary upper hand, that's all. Newcastle fans may claim that more FA Cup triumphs and European campaigns over their historic rivals proves superiority, as well as a better head-to-head overall record at first-team competitive level, whilst those of a red-and-white persuasion may claim that six top-flight League Championships is the clincher.

Irrespective of what the clubs' fans think, it is undeniable that both clubs should be at the heart of English football. They should both be winning trophies and satisfying the unreasonable demands of their supporters. For some reason they aren't but perhaps one day a magic formula will be found.

How have teams that included modern-day legends such as Alan Shearer and Niall Quinn never even won, say, a League Cup? You tell me.

However, if you aren't prepared to try to match the demands of the fans then don't play for one of our teams. Don't kiss the badge unless you mean it. Don't manage them if you can't handle it. Don't give excuses, neither club's supporters want to hear them. Just give us the teams that the supporters of both clubs deserve.

If you are a true football person and you want to enter the world of northeast football then embrace it and go for it. I doubt you will be disappointed. Our region lives and breathes the game – it's still very much a hotbed of soccer.

Ha'way the Lads!

Paul Days, May 2012

Newcastle United v Sunderland AFC – Tyne-Wear League Derby Matches Only

Game N°	Season	Date	Comp	Home	Score			Away	Venue	Att
1	1898/1899	24/12/1898	FL1	Sunderland	2	v	3	Newcastle Utd	RP	30,000
4	1899/1900	28/4/1900	FL1	Sunderland	1	v	2	Newcastle Utd	RP	22,000
5	1900/1901	6/10/1900	FL1	Sunderland	1	v	1	Newcastle Utd	RP	28,688
8	1901/1902	31/3/1902	FL1	Sunderland	0	v	0	Newcastle Utd	RP	34,819
9	1902/1903	27/12/1902	FL1	Sunderland	0	v	0	Newcastle Utd	RP	26,000
12	1903/1904	1/1/1904	FL1	Sunderland	1	v	1	Newcastle Utd	RP	30,000
13	1904/1905	24/12/1904	FL1	Sunderland	3	v	1	Newcastle Utd	RP	30,000
15	1905/1906	2/9/1905	FL1	Sunderland	3	v	2	Newcastle Utd	RP	30,000
18	1906/1907	20/3/1907	FL1	Sunderland	2	v	0	Newcastle Utd	RP	32,000
19	1907/1908	21/12/1907	FL1	Sunderland	2	v	4	Newcastle Utd	RP	30,000
22	1908/1909	10/4/1909	FL1	Sunderland	3	v	1	Newcastle Utd	RP	30,000
23	1909/1910	18/9/1909	FL1	Sunderland	0	v	2	Newcastle Utd	RP	35,000
25	1910/1911	1/9/1910	FL1	Sunderland	2	v	1	Newcastle Utd	RP	30,000
27	1911/1912	14/10/1911	FL1	Sunderland	1	v	2	Newcastle Utd	RP	20,000
30	1912/1913	28/12/1912	FL1	Sunderland	2	v	0	Newcastle Utd	RP	35,000
31	1913/1914	6/9/1913	FL1	Sunderland	1	v	2	Newcastle Utd	RP	45,000
34	1914/1915	26/12/1914	FL1	Sunderland	2	v	4	Newcastle Utd	RP	20,000
35	1919/1920	22/11/1919	FL1	Sunderland	2	v	0	Newcastle Utd	RP	47,148
38	1920/1921	16/10/1920	FL1	Sunderland	0	v	2	Newcastle Utd	RP	38,000
40	1921/1922	26/11/1921	FL1	Sunderland	0	v	0	Newcastle Utd	RP	49,483
42	1922/1923	11/11/1922	FL1	Sunderland	2	v	0	Newcastle Utd	RP	50,000
43	1923/1924	15/12/1923	FL1	Sunderland	3	v	2	Newcastle Utd	RP	45,000
45	1924/1925	18/10/1924	FL1	Sunderland	1	v	1	Newcastle Utd	RP	55,642
48	1925/1926	27/2/1926	FL1	Sunderland	2	v	2	Newcastle Utd	RP	36,000
49	1926/1927	30/10/1926	FL1	Sunderland	2	v	0	Newcastle Utd	RP	30,000
52	1927/1928	17/3/1928	FL1	Sunderland	1	v	1	Newcastle Utd	RP	40,071
53	1928/1929	27/10/1928	FL1	Sunderland	5	v	2	Newcastle Utd	RP	50,519
55	1929/1930	19/10/1929	FL1	Sunderland	1	v	0	Newcastle Utd	RP	58,519
57	1930/1931	22/11/1930	FL1	Sunderland	5	v	0	Newcastle Utd	RP	24,120
59	1931/1932	28/11/1931	FL1	Sunderland	1	v	4	Newcastle Utd	RP	34,580
61	1932/1933	26/11/1932	FL1	Sunderland	0	v	2	Newcastle Utd	RP	40,000
64	1933/1934	3/3/1934	FL1	Sunderland	2	v	0	Newcastle Utd	RP	31,776
65	1948/1949	9/10/1948	FL1	Sunderland	1	v	1	Newcastle Utd	RP	51,399
68	1949/1950	4/3/1950	FL1	Sunderland	2	v	2	Newcastle Utd	RP	68,004
70	1950/1951	26/3/1951	FL1	Sunderland	2	v	1	Newcastle Utd	RP	55,150
71	1951/1952	25/12/1951	FL1	Sunderland	1	v	4	Newcastle Utd	RP	52,274
74	1952/1953	17/9/1952	FL1	Sunderland	0	v	2	Newcastle Utd	RP	59,665

76	1953/1954	19/12/1953	FL1	Sunderland	1	v	1	Newcastle Utd	RP	49,922
77	1954/1955	9/10/1954	FL1	Sunderland	4	v	2	Newcastle Utd	RP	66,654
79	1955/1956	26/12/1955	FL1	Sunderland	1	v	6	Newcastle Utd	RP	55,723
81	1956/1957	25/8/1956	FL1	Sunderland	1	v	2	Newcastle Utd	RP	51,032
83	1957/1958	21/9/1957	FL1	Sunderland	2	v	0	Newcastle Utd	RP	45,718
86	1961/1962	21/4/1962	FL2	Sunderland	3	v	0	Newcastle Utd	RP	57,666
88	1962/1963	2/3/1963	FL2	Sunderland	0	v	0	Newcastle Utd	RP	62,420
89	1963/1964	9/10/1963	FL2	Sunderland	2	v	1	Newcastle Utd	RP	56,903
91	1965/1966	3/1/1966	FL1	Sunderland	2	v	0	Newcastle Utd	RP	54,668
94	1966/1967	4/3/1967	FL1	Sunderland	3	v	0	Newcastle Utd	RP	50,442
96	1967/1968	30/12/1967	FL1	Sunderland	3	v	3	Newcastle Utd	RP	46,030
97	1968/1969	31/8/1968	FL1	Sunderland	1	v	1	Newcastle Utd	RP	49,428
100	1969/1970	27/3/1970	FL1	Sunderland	1	v	1	Newcastle Utd	RP	51,950
102	1976/1977	8/4/1977	FL1	Sunderland	2	v	2	Newcastle Utd	RP	46,056
103	1978/1979	14/10/1978	FL2	Sunderland	1	v	1	Newcastle Utd	RP	35,405
106	1979/1980	5/4/1980	FL2	Sunderland	1	v	0	Newcastle Utd	RP	41,752
108	1984/1985	8/4/1985	FL1	Sunderland	0	v	0	Newcastle Utd	RP	28,246
109	1989/1990	24/9/1989	FL2	Sunderland	0	v	0	Newcastle Utd	RP	29,449
111	1991/1992	17/11/1991	FL2	Sunderland	1	v	1	Newcastle Utd	RP	29,224
113	1992/1993	18/10/1992	FL1	Sunderland	1	v	2	Newcastle Utd	RP	28,098
115	1996/1997	4/9/1996	FAPL	Sunderland	1	v	2	Newcastle Utd	RP	22,037
118	1999/2000	5/2/2000	FAPL	Sunderland	2	v	2	Newcastle Utd	SOL	42,192
120	2000/2001	21/4/2001	FAPL	Sunderland	1	v	1	Newcastle Utd	SOL	48,277
122	2001/2002	24/2/2002	FAPL	Sunderland	0	v	1	Newcastle Utd	SOL	48,290
124	2002/2003	26/4/2003	FAPL	Sunderland	0	v	1	Newcastle Utd	SOL	45,067
126	2005/2006	17/4/2006	FAPL	Sunderland	1	v	4	Newcastle Utd	SOL	40,032
127	2007/2008	10/11/2007	FAPL	Sunderland	1	v	1	Newcastle Utd	SOL	47,701
129	2008/2009	25/10/2008	FAPL	Sunderland	2	v	1	Newcastle Utd	SOL	47,936
132	2010/2011	16/1/2011	FAPL	Sunderland	1	v	1	Newcastle Utd	SOL	47,864
133	2011/2012	21/8/2011	FAPL	Sunderland	0	v	1	Newcastle Utd	SOL	47,751

NEWCASTLE UNITED vs SUNDERLAND

Game N°	Season	Date	Comp	Home	Score			Away	Venue	Att
2	1898/1899	22/4/1899	FL1	Newcastle Utd	0	v	1	Sunderland	SJP	25,000
3	1899/1900	23/12/1899	FL1	Newcastle Utd	2	v	4	Sunderland	SJP	19,129
6	1900/1901	24/4/1901	FL1	Newcastle Utd	0	v	2	Sunderland	SJP	18,694
7	1901/1902	28/9/1901	FL1	Newcastle Utd	0	v	1	Sunderland	SJP	23,330
10	1902/1903	25/4/1903	FL1	Newcastle Utd	1	v	0	Sunderland	SJP	27,500
11	1903/1904	26/12/1903	FL1	Newcastle Utd	1	v	3	Sunderland	SJP	25,000
14	1904/1905	22/4/1905	FL1	Newcastle Utd	1	v	3	Sunderland	SJP	30,000
16	1905/1906	30/12/1905	FL1	Newcastle Utd	1	v	1	Sunderland	SJP	56,000
17	1906/1907	1/9/1906	FL1	Newcastle Utd	4	v	2	Sunderland	SJP	56,375
20	1907/1908	18/4/1908	FL1	Newcastle Utd	1	v	3	Sunderland	SJP	50,000
21	1908/1909	5/12/1908	FL1	Newcastle Utd	1	v	9	Sunderland	SJP	60,000
24	1909/1910	13/4/1910	FL1	Newcastle Utd	1	v	0	Sunderland	SJP	40,000
26	1910/1911	19/11/1910	FL1	Newcastle Utd	1	v	1	Sunderland	SJP	57,416
28	1911/1912	17/2/1912	FL1	Newcastle Utd	3	v	1	Sunderland	SJP	45,000
29	1912/1913	7/9/1912	FL1	Newcastle Utd	1	v	1	Sunderland	SJP	54,215
32	1913/1914	27/12/1913	FL1	Newcastle Utd	2	v	1	Sunderland	SJP	50,000
33	1914/1915	25/12/1914	FL1	Newcastle Utd	2	v	5	Sunderland	SJP	40,000
36	1919/1920	29/11/1919	FL1	Newcastle Utd	2	v	3	Sunderland	SJP	61,761
37	1920/1921	9/10/1920	FL1	Newcastle Utd	6	v	1	Sunderland	SJP	58,016
39	1921/1922	19/11/1921	FL1	Newcastle Utd	2	v	2	Sunderland	SJP	46,000
41	1922/1923	4/11/1922	FL1	Newcastle Utd	2	v	1	Sunderland	SJP	60,000
44	1923/1924	22/12/1923	FL1	Newcastle Utd	0	v	2	Sunderland	SJP	50,000
46	1924/1925	21/2/1925	FL1	Newcastle Utd	2	v	0	Sunderland	SJP	52,000
47	1925/1926	17/10/1925	FL1	Newcastle Utd	0	v	0	Sunderland	SJP	52,000
50	1926/1927	19/3/1927	FL1	Newcastle Utd	1	v	0	Sunderland	SJP	67,211
51	1927/1928	5/11/1927	FL1	Newcastle Utd	3	v	1	Sunderland	SJP	44,780
54	1928/1929	9/3/1929	FL1	Newcastle Utd	4	v	3	Sunderland	SJP	65,838
56	1929/1930	22/2/1930	FL1	Newcastle Utd	3	v	0	Sunderland	SJP	49,304
58	1930/1931	28/3/1931	FL1	Newcastle Utd	2	v	0	Sunderland	SJP	38,000
60	1931/1932	9/4/1932	FL1	Newcastle Utd	1	v	2	Sunderland	SJP	45,000
62	1932/1933	8/4/1933	FL1	Newcastle Utd	0	v	1	Sunderland	SJP	42,000
63	1933/1934	21/10/1933	FL1	Newcastle Utd	2	v	1	Sunderland	SJP	45,000
66	1948/1949	5/3/1949	FL1	Newcastle Utd	2	v	1	Sunderland	SJP	58,250
67	1949/1950	15/10/1949	FL1	Newcastle Utd	2	v	2	Sunderland	SJP	55,000
69	1950/1951	23/3/1951	FL1	Newcastle Utd	2	v	2	Sunderland	SJP	62,173
72	1951/1952	26/12/1951	FL1	Newcastle Utd	2	v	2	Sunderland	SJP	63,665
73	1952/1953	10/9/1952	FL1	Newcastle Utd	2	v	2	Sunderland	SJP	60,727
75	1953/1954	22/8/1953	FL1	Newcastle Utd	2	v	1	Sunderland	SJP	58,516
78	1954/1955	26/2/1955	FL1	Newcastle Utd	1	v	2	Sunderland	SJP	62,835
80	1955/1956	27/12/1955	FL1	Newcastle Utd	3	v	1	Sunderland	SJP	61,058
82	1956/1957	22/12/1956	FL1	Newcastle Utd	6	v	2	Sunderland	SJP	29,727
84	1957/1958	1/2/1958	FL1	Newcastle Utd	2	v	2	Sunderland	SJP	47,500

85	1961/1962	2/12/1961	FL2	Newcastle Utd	2	v	2	Sunderland	SJP	53,991
87	1962/1963	13/10/1962	FL2	Newcastle Utd	1	v	1	Sunderland	SJP	62,262
90	1963/1964	14/3/1964	FL2	Newcastle Utd	1	v	0	Sunderland	SJP	27,341
92	1965/1966	5/3/1966	FL1	Newcastle Utd	2	v	0	Sunderland	SJP	52,051
93	1966/1967	29/10/1966	FL1	Newcastle Utd	0	v	3	Sunderland	SJP	57,643
95	1967/1968	26/12/1967	FL1	Newcastle Utd	2	v	1	Sunderland	SJP	59,579
98	1968/1969	22/3/1969	FL1	Newcastle Utd	1	v	1	Sunderland	SJP	48,588
99	1969/1970	8/11/1969	FL1	Newcastle Utd	3	v	0	Sunderland	SJP	56,317
101	1976/1977	27/12/1976	FL1	Newcastle Utd	2	v	0	Sunderland	SJP	50,048
104	1978/1979	24/2/1979	FL2	Newcastle Utd	1	v	4	Sunderland	SJP	34,733
105	1979/1980	1/1/1980	FL2	Newcastle Utd	3	v	1	Sunderland	SJP	38,322
107	1984/1985	1/1/1985	FL1	Newcastle Utd	3	v	1	Sunderland	SJP	36,821
110	1989/1990	4/2/1990	FL2	Newcastle Utd	1	v	1	Sunderland	SJP	31,572
112	1991/1992	29/3/1992	FL2	Newcastle Utd	1	v	0	Sunderland	SJP	30,306
114	1992/1993	25/4/1993	FL1	Newcastle Utd	1	v	0	Sunderland	SJP	30,364
116	1996/1997	5/4/1997	FAPL	Newcastle Utd	1	v	1	Sunderland	SJP	36,582
117	1999/2000	25/8/1999	FAPL	Newcastle Utd	1	v	2	Sunderland	SJP	36,420
119	2000/2001	18/11/2000	FAPL	Newcastle Utd	1	v	2	Sunderland	SJP	52,030
121	2001/2002	25/8/2001	FAPL	Newcastle Utd	1	v	1	Sunderland	SJP	52,021
123	2002/2003	22/9/2002	FAPL	Newcastle Utd	2	v	0	Sunderland	SJP	52,181
125	2005/2006	23/10/2005	FAPL	Newcastle Utd	3	v	2	Sunderland	SJP	52,302
128	2007/2008	20/4/2008	FAPL	Newcastle Utd	2	v	0	Sunderland	SJP	52,305
130	2008/2009	1/2/2009	FAPL	Newcastle Utd	1	v	1	Sunderland	SJP	52,084
131	2010/2011	31/10/2010	FAPL	Newcastle Utd	5	v	1	Sunderland	SJP	51,988
134	2011/2012	4/3/2012	FAPL	Newcastle Utd	1	v	1	Sunderland	SJP	52,388

Team	W	D	L	F	A
Newcastle Utd	51	42	41	208	196
Sunderland	41	42	51	196	208

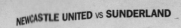